Project *Cheers*

Project Cheers

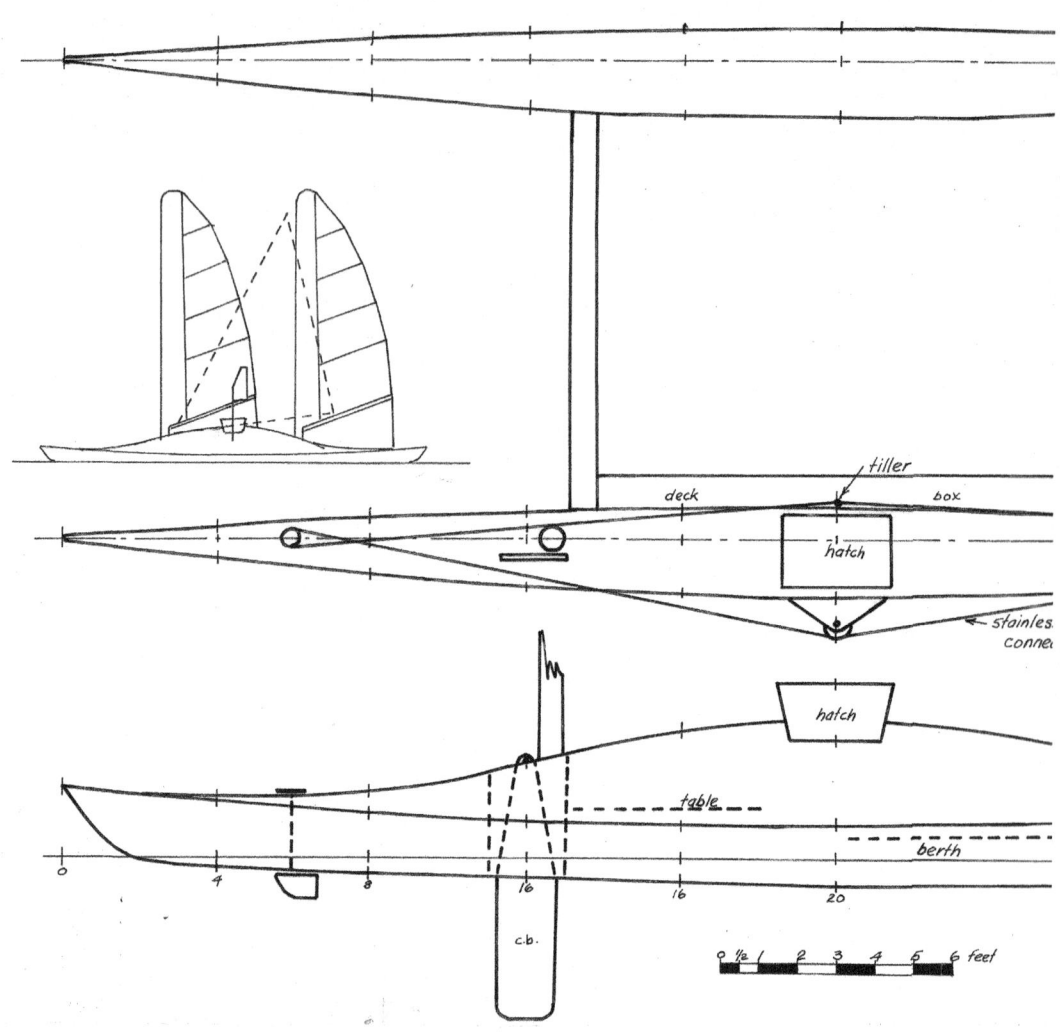

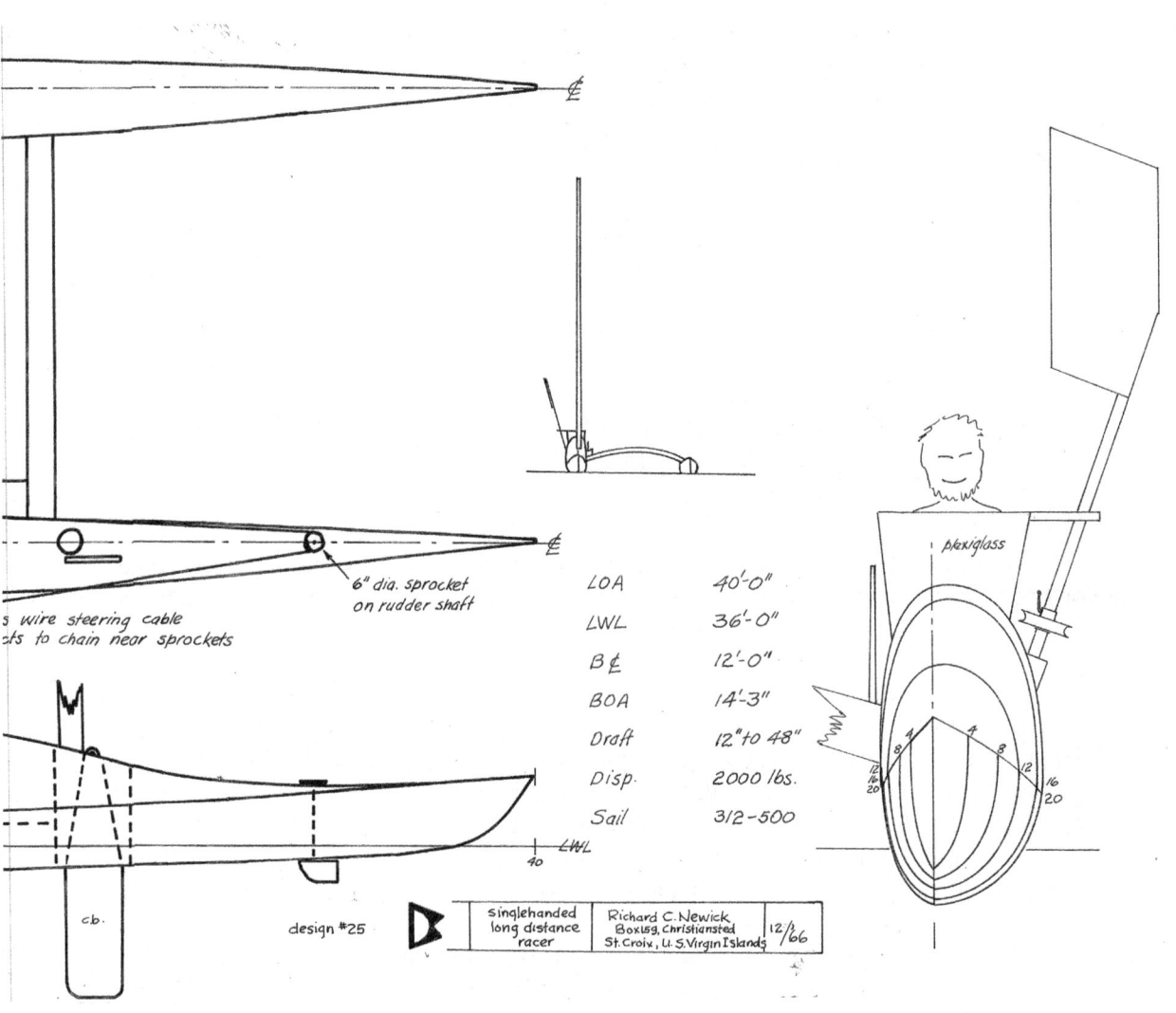

The initial concept of Cheers: it is interesting to compare this with the final form as illustrated in the back of the book.

Project Cheers

©T. Follett, R. Newick, J. Morris 1969

Project _Cheers_ was first published in Great Britain in 1969 by Adlard Coles Ltd. 3 Upper James St, Golden Square, London W1.
First printed in Great Britain by
Ebenezer Baylis and Son Ltd
The Trinity Press, Worcester, and London
SBN 229 63900 3 as a hard cover with jacket

This revised edition of Project _Cheers_ is published in 2016, with permission from the copyright heirs and the original publisher, by Russell & Ashlyn Brown;
Port Townsend Watercraft LLC
PO Box 1875 Port Townsend WA 98368, USA
ISBN-13 978-1523961160 / ISBN-10 1523961163

EDITOR'S NOTE-
This second edition includes the original British spelling and the original 'voice' of the three authors. This was the consensus of the copyright heirs; to keep the book as close to the original as possible.
   The editor here-in also apologizes for any poor quality of some photos. Not all of the original photos were found and saved digitally. Big thanks go to the copyright heirs for providing as many of the originals as they did and in general for their support and assistance in making this second edition of Project _Cheers_ a reality. Thanks also go out to Bill Barker of the Mariner's Museum in Newport News and to Michael Schacht for their assistance.
   A webpage has been created with photos, additional information and links to other websites for those who wish to dig deeper into this history and relevant events since 1969.
   Please visit: http://www.cheersdicknewick.wordpress.com
   With the America's Cup of recent years fully taking advantage of multihulls, and multihulls breaking records at an astonishing pace, a renewed interest in the proa concept is taking root. The editor and publisher of this edition of Project _Cheers_, along with the copyright heirs, embarked on this project with the intention to honor Dick Newick, Jim Morris, and Tom Follett for their vision and perseverance demonstrated in the pages that follow.
-_Ashlyn E. Brown_

Cover photos by Dick Newick, author portraits by Fritz Henle.

Project *Cheers*

A new concept in boat design

by Tom Follett, Dick Newick and Jim Morris
With many photographs by Fritz Henle

Project Cheers

Port Townsend Watercraft LLC, USA

Dedicated to Pris Follett, Pat Newick and Tootie Morris

Project Cheers

Contents

Plates, 10
Forward by H.G. ('Blondie') Hasler, 11
Preface by Ian Major, 13
Introduction, 15

Part I - Organising the organised - by Jim Morris, 17
The Decision is taken, 19
Work to be done, 27
Final arrangements, 35
An anxious wait, 41
Gosport to Plymouth, 49
Acceptance at last and a good start, 63
A beautiful third place, 75
    Postscript

Part II - The story according to Tom Follett, 83
Early trials, 85
St Croix to Gosport, 113
The race and some subsequent musings, 129

Part III - Design & construction by Dick Newick, 143
The idea is born, 147
Cheers is built, 157
First trials and the race, 171

Plates

1. *Cheers* under construction, with Bernard Rhodes,
2. *Cheers* under construction showing lamination of the aka,
3. *Cheers* under construction showing 12mm ply bulkheads,
4. Walford Galloway,
5. Dick Newick makes some last minute adjustments to the mast,
6. The Launch.
7. *Cheers*!
8. The team prepares *Cheers* for her first sail,
9. Capsize test before sponson was fitted,
10. The same capsize test,
11. Tom Follett prior to his first solo excursion,
12. Tom Follett on his first long solo trial,
13. *Cheers* during early trials off St. Croix,
14. *Cheers* on an early trial,
15. During early trials, showing light weather foresail,
16. Close-up showing the cockpit layout and the netting,
17. *Cheers* showing her paces during trials,
18. *Cheers* in action during trials,
19. A close fetch at high speed during trials,
20. Sponson and anti-dive plates,
21. One of the anti-dive plates,
22. Tom Follett leaving Christiansted for England,
23. *Cheers* alongside her tender *Andiamo* at Millbay Dock, Plymouth,
24. The opposite end of windward hull,
25. Tom Follett's quarters in the windward hull,
26. Home after the race,
27. The contestants in the 1968 Single-Handed Transatlantic Race,
28. *Cheers* racing with Newick's third trimaran,

Forward

The 1968 *Cheers* project will stand as a perfect example of the sort of thing that a Single-Handed Transatlantic Race was designed to encourage. I don't know which to admire the most: the extreme un-orthodoxy of the boat's conception, or the strength and simplicity of her construction; or perhaps her wild good looks; or the efficiency with which she was tested, modified, re-tested, and then proof-tested in that extraordinary passage from St. Croix to Gosport; or Tom Follett's impeccable seamanship allied to his rudimentary ocean-going inventory. I think most great seamen have chosen to use a minimum of equipment: we have another Slocum here.

Next we can appreciate the team's sportsmanship and good manners in their dealings with the Royal Western Yacht Club, and for that matter the responsible attitude of Jack Odling-Smee and his hard pressed Race Committee in first rejecting this apparently frivolous entry, and then being able to change their minds gracefully when presented with fresh evidence.

Cheers is really a very small boat, as anyone who has got into her cabin can testify. The route which she took, or was forced to take, is in my opinion a slow one which would normally add several days to any boat's time. I think she did superbly to finish third, and to better Tabarly's 1964 record passage.

Every part of the *Cheers* project seems to have set a standard of excellence that we can now look on and marvel at.

H.G. Hasler
Curdridge
Hampshire
3rd June 1969

Project Cheers

Preface

This is a story of simple human endeavour. It is unusual in many ways. A new concept in boat design; a double crossing of the Atlantic -- St Croix, US Virgin Islands to England; the Single-Handed Transatlantic Race to Newport, Rhode Island; thence the return journey to St Croix, -- nine thousand miles in a total sailing time of 68 days at an average speed of 5½ knots. To this add a unique exercise in functional, spartan living at sea, plus the attainment of directional stability without vane steering gear. Finally, most remarkable of all, the word by word extraction of the skipper's story; the Tom Follett story.

I debriefed Tom when he arrived in Portsmouth, England, after his superb 28-day sail from St Croix. I had prepared a detailed questionnaire and expected to learn much. As it turned out, I learnt practically nothing, except, that it was 'a good sail'. Getting the story out of Tom Follett was like questioning a brave and well trained prisoner during World War II. It reminded me of my abortive interrogation of some Italian Frogmen who had successfully raided Algiers harbour during the TORCH phase of World War II. I learned from them absolutely nothing ---except that they were skilled and very brave men for whom I had an enormous admiration.

So with Tom Follett. I talked with him after all three voyages in this Transatlantic saga. I learned remarkably little. Nothing but a diffident, irreducibly shortened, précis of the whole story, which when added up pointed to 'a good sail' and 'a good boat'. But as he pursued this exercise in staggering modesty, I came to like and admire, and, I suppose, envy him, more and more.

Tom Follett is the undoubted hero of this adventure. I say this, notwithstanding Jim Morris's unique powers of leadership and administration (without him I doubt whether *Cheers* would have departed

St Croix); and Dick Newick's inspired, revolutionary, well built racing machine of great beauty; and the infinitely great contribution of understanding, patience, and charming assistance from beginning to end of the three wives, Pris, Tootie and Pat, of these wonderful American friends of mine.

And what was all this in aid of? What was the driving force? The classic answer is that if you don't instinctively understand why people do such things, then nobody else can explain. Maybe this is good enough. But I, as a believer, albeit a somewhat rusty one, would like to suggest, if not a reason why, a reason for. I'd like to think that Project *Cheers* entry in the 3rd Single-Handed Transatlantic Race was regarded as a good example of what men can do in the newly found age of leisure. Instead of the tragic bitterness which has erupted at the confluence of the age of leisure and the age of the concrete jungle, that there was hope and inspiration. Man can pursue his leisure creatively. That for every one man who races alone across the Atlantic, some hundreds, thousands of men and women will be inspired to climb their own, subjective, coveted and very private mountain. Whether this be learning to glide, cycling across Africa, canoeing down the Rhine, or simply sailing their dinghy out of sight of land.

And in so doing discover the few remaining aspects of wilderness in our modern world, and the regeneration and enlightenment, and closer to true Godliness, that only such pure adventure brings.

As for me, just being a honorary member of Project *Cheers* was truly inspiring. I was hooked. The excitement of chasing the mighty dollar in the Klondike of Caribbean real estate, pales by comparison. Before the last faint rumours of youth fade in my veins, maybe it's not late to bail out, and tipping my cap to Tom Follett, do likewise.

Ian Major,
St Thomas,
23rd September 1968.

Introduction

It isn't every day an unusual boat moves off the drawing board and into the water and is more than moderately successful. This is the story of one such unusual boat.

Cheers is her name. She's a proa although there are some differences between her and the boats built by the Polynesians. She is called a 'proa' because one hull is always to windward or, if you like, another hull is always to leeward. She differs from the usual idea of a proa in that her two hulls are identical below the sheerline and, perhaps, because of her schooner rig.

Getting the boat off the drawing board and into the water was a bit of a project. Several people ended up being involved but three more so than the rest and these three will contribute to the tale.

Dick Newick who designed and built her, will take care of the details of the boat, her construction and her subsequent modifications. Jim Morris ran the project and he will explain how it was organized and how it operated and he'll also tell about some of the other people who became involved as time went on. Tom Follett was the crew and he will discuss the trials at sea and the fairly long trips she made before being temporarily laid up in St. Croix around the 20th July 1968.

The 1968 Single-Handed Transatlantic Race is part of it all and there will be something said about that. In fact, there will be rather a lot said about the race since it was because of this the whole thing got started.

The yacht was entered in the race after some difficulty with approval from the Race Committee. She was entered as a yacht from the US Virgin Islands since that was where she was built, that is where her designer lives and both Morris and Follett consider the islands as a sort of second home.

The Virgin Islands are a rather larger group extending for about 40 miles in a general east-west direction. St. Croix is considered as part of the Virgin Islands but is stuck off by itself about 35 miles to the south of St. Thomas. Its largest town is Christiansted with a fairly good harbor well protected by reefs, which is ideal for yachts except during hurricane season.

Some of the islands are British and some are part of the USA. This is good territory for experimenting with yacht design with excellent weather nearly all the time. Winds are constant as is the temperature. The water is warm and clear and the long passages are often rough enough to be interesting. A nice place to live and a nice place to build a boat.

Part one

Organising the organised

Project Cheers

Chapter one

The decision is taken

It was a glorious day in Colorado on 15th April 1967. One of our usual late Spring snowstorms had just passed through, lacing the countryside with white, and now the skies were a magnificent blue and the sun shone brilliantly on the front range of the Rockies.

I had no idea what this day would bring, but I was not to be left wondering for long. In fact, I shall never forget the letter left by the postman as he hollered 'Hope it's good news', because it came from Dick Newick in the Virgin Islands. Now when Dick writes from St Croix it is always by airmail (otherwise it takes six months), but when a letter comes from him marked 'Special Delivery' then you can't help but expect the worst.

In the event it was good news all right, depending on which way you look at it and on how many mothers, mothers-in-law and families you might have. Dick had simply seen fit to spend the extra 'stipend' for special delivery to advise me that he and Tom Follett had put their heads together and decided that the three of us should take part in the Single-Handed Transatlantic Race in 1968!

Naturally I knew something about the race before Dick wrote, firstly because I had read with great interest Eric Tabarly's book, *Lonely Victory, Atlantic Race 1964*, and secondly because Dick had shown me some sketches when I was in St Croix earlier in the year of a boat he was proposing to design for his good friend John Goodwin of South Africa. As I now understood it, John was very interested in skippering Dick's boat but was unable at the time to raise the funds. In essence, therefore, Dick had a boat--a potential winner; he had a skipper in Tom Follett, a hardy and knowledgeable man of the sea, but at that point things stopped.

Out here when someone is picked to be an 'angel' he is sometimes referred to, disrespectfully, as a 'mullet'. I want to make it quite clear that at no time and in no way did I ever feel that Tom and Dick were inviting me to join the group for the sole purpose of raising cash. My wife Tootie and I still find it impossible though to come up with any logical explanation as to why we became so excited and thrilled at the prospect of becoming part of the team. Well, there's no reason in the world why we should try and justify our decision to participate. We just made it and a wire to that effect went off to St Croix--Project 68, as we then called it, was born.

If ever there was a team effort likely to succeed Project 68 had all the elements, physically, mentally and personality-wise. The key-note was compatibility and I challenge anyone to find fault with the compatibility of the three families comprising Project 68. It's all right to say you will do a thing, but then to perform and succeed is quite another matter. Actually, this is what was so thrilling throughout the entire undertaking. One thing is for sure, three men getting their heads together and going off into the wind might not be unusual, but to have their respective brides equally enthusiastic is an accomplishment indeed.

I have known Dick Newick in the Virgin Islands socially and in business for many years. One thing he has in plenty is ideas and when it comes to putting them on paper in the form of a multi-hull design he is, in my book, unchallenged. As for Tom Follett and his wife Pris, Tootie and I have been privileged several times to share their wonderful company in the islands and over a period had developed a great fondness for them both. There was no conflict, thank goodness, of personalities, no individual desire for achievement, but rather a unified spirit in an undertaking which, from the start, held for all of us great moments of elation, many tremendous disappointments and at least one moment when we almost had to scrub the entire project.

At the time the decision was made for the triumvirate to step up and be counted, Dick was at St Croix. Tom Follett was on the high seas delivering a yacht from St Thomas to New York and I was in Denver, Colorado. Though by now we were in complete agreement I thought it was time for the three minds to meet as soon as possible and at a location most convenient to us all.

On 12th May 1967, Dick and I flew to Miami and we all met in Tom's apartment--(would you believe 2855 Tigertail Avenue, Apartment 306?). It was there that we formulated the final concept of the yacht in some detail, delineated areas of responsibility, worked out a time schedule and, perhaps, most important of all, a philosophy under which Project 68 would operate.

This took three days, intermingled with poolside jocularity, cuisine by the master, Tom Follett, and harmonious interludes of guitar playing by Tom and Pris.

Before our meeting Dick and Tom had pretty much decided that the original drawings that Dick had made were in principal OK and to this day our boat appears almost exactly as in Dick's first designs.

As far as the areas of responsibility were concerned, the immediate 'proof of the pudding' fell on Dick's shoulders in transforming the design from paper into a potential race winner. This was no easy task when one knows that there was little or no place to go for advice or help. However, there were suggestions—many, almost too many! It was no easy task when there was no other Boat in the world that looked or sailed like our proposed craft. Perhaps more significantly however, to build a boat in the Virgin Islands is, to say the least, no cinch. The organisation of available manpower and the location of materials and equipment, let alone delivering them to the site, was a challenge for the most organised and a guarantee for the development of an ulcer. What is more Follett or Morris could be of little help in Miami or Denver.

It was agreed that Tom's area of responsibility would take full shape from the moment our yacht was launched and last until the end of the Race. He was to have the task of campaigning the boat, of making suggestions for alterations in the design as well as the sails and, of course, sail in the Race. Little did we know at that time that getting to the start would mean that Tom would have to sail the boat to England!

As for myself, well, perhaps I bought myself a job, but my task was to organise the organised--a job which if offered again, would be accepted eagerly and with no concern, but only if it were with shipmates Newick and Follett.

Before Dick and I left Miami to pursue the problems at hand, the triumvirate came up with a 'letter of mutual understanding' and perhaps the essence of this understanding is best captured in the last paragraph:

'It is mutually agreed by all the participating members of Project 68 that individually and collectively, every effort will be made to fulfill the project's main objective, winning of the 1968 Single-Handed Trans-Atlantic Race, always keeping in mind the desire for Tom's safety as well as quality in design, construction and the sailing of the boat throughout the campaign. No member of the project should ever feel restrained to discuss, disagree, or make suggestions as he wishes, even should the area in question not be his direct responsibility. The project will be carried on in the desire that all participate, that nothing should be compromised with regard to quality of material used or equipment purchased--that we go first class, but paying our own way 100%--no sponsorship of any kind, no discounts taken if by doing so we would be beholden to someone at a later date.'

We were to undertake the adventure in hand in good taste and we would conduct ourselves so as to be a credit to our country and the project throughout.

I am eager to record the proposed time schedule for I am sure that anyone so involved in a project of this nature cannot help but be amazed at how closely we held to the schedule at hand. Quoting from item five of our letter of mutual understanding dated 24th May 1967;

5 · Proposed Time Schedule:

Ordering of lumber--May 1967
Plug started--Late May, early June
Launching--Late October 1967--We came close but no cigar. Launched December 12th 1967
Testing and Trials--November and December, 1967 and January through March, 1968. This is to be accomplished in the area of St Croix, the Caribbean, and the Atlantic.
Shipping by freighter to England-April 1968 (We may have to sail to England).

Final preparations for the Race in and around Plymouth, England--two or three weeks prior to the Race, May of 1968. (We didn't even know when the Race started.)

Finish of the Race--hopefully May 1968 Newport, Rhode Island, U.S.A.

You see, we didn't even know whether the race started in May or June but at least we were vain enough to think we would finish in the same month as we started. All of this was finally accomplished but in those early days there was a very busy schedule ahead to say the least, with visits to New York and Connecticut to visit friends in the field of design, to start ordering materials and finally to keep a promise to our respective families to give them a month-long sail from St Croix to Grenada and back in *Ay Ay*; a 40 ft day sailing cat designed by Dick Newick.

Well it was time to move on and when Dick and I said farewell to Tom and Pris there was a wonderful feeling among us all that unity of purpose had been achieved. Little did we realise that for many months, in excess of a year in fact, we would be, so to speak, bedfellows.

Under our belts we had the achievement of having given birth to Project 68, the philosophy of how we would pursue the adventure, a complete meeting of the minds on areas of responsibility, and in addition we had spent the first dollars of Project 68 for the African mahogany veneer which would be the basic construction material for the boat.

By now it was the latter part of May 1967, and I guess that enough progress had been made for us to have been satisfied rather than concerned as to whether or not we were on schedule.

At that particular moment the matter which seemed to be of the greatest importance was whether or not the masts should be constructed out of some alloy. I guess for a matter of two or three days we had seriously thought about using aluminum, perhaps even some form of standard lamp post. Eventually it was decided that we knew little or nothing about the structural strength or compatibility of materials when it came to using an alloy with wood. We did, however, know a great deal about the stress and strain qualities of wood; we were familiar in how to work with it; we were comfortable in using it, and thus our first problem was solved. All parts of the hulls, the crossmember, the masts and booms would be of some form of wood.

We had asked Tom to be the project contact with the Race Committee of the Royal Western Yacht Club of England. It was Tom, then, who first forwarded the check in payment of the entry fee, publicly stating our intentions for the first time, that we wished to be considered as an entrant in the race. Dick in the mean time had sent off working drawings to the committee so as to keep them well advised as to our plans.

It might be significant at this point to comment briefly on our genuine desire to keep the Race Committee informed as to our intentions and our progress. Somewhere along the way we had received the official 'Rules and Conditions of Entry' for the race. I think that the members of the project team could recite the various paragraphs by memory but a portion of paragraph 14 especially will never be forgotten:

> 'Eligibility of yachts--Yachts of any size or type may enter, subject to the decision of the organisers. It is not their desire to exclude yachts solely on the grounds of unconventional type or design, but a person contemplating entering an extreme type, either by reason of its size or other features, would be well advised to give particulars of the yacht at an early stage so as to avoid later disappointment.'

Our proposed size, we felt, was not extreme, but we certainly didn't have to stretch our imagination to appreciate fully that our design might be considered unconventional. With these words ringing in our ears and gnawing at us continually, we established the philosophy that we would keep the race committee as well informed as possible to our intentions, our progress, our failures and achievements and at no time would we hide a thing.

I am confident that this was the only course we could have taken, and, my, how successful the results were. Admittedly there were times throughout the entire course of the project that perhaps we would have wished we had been able to compromise with our philosophy under which we did 'Report in' to the race committee.

It wasn't long before we were to have our first doubts for we received a letter dated 25th July 1967 from Captain Terrance W. B. Shaw, Secretary (Sailing) of the Royal Western Yacht Club of England. It was in this communiqué that the first of many questions was to be asked about our project and it was from this first letter that we knew we had to sell ourselves to the Committee and this would not be an easy task.

'The Committee are not altogether happy with the design, and in particular we see the possibility of being taken aback while the crew is resting below. Would you please explain to us how, in such a condition, the yacht is prevented from capsizing?'

It is interesting to itemise the dates of communications between the project team and the race committee:

18th August 1967-Entry fee returned by Captain Shaw to Tom.

22nd August 1967-Captain Shaw responded to my letter regarding accommodation and general area of the starting line.

1st September 1967-Dick Newick composed a detailed letter earnestly trying to answer in detail questions raised by the Race Committee. By now we were a little disturbed.

5th September 1967-Tom wrote the Race Committee about having seen *Cheers* in St Croix during construction and tried to evidence his great satisfaction with what he saw.

Ah--a month or so without any discouraging word. . . .

20th October 1967 Captain Shaw wrote on behalf of the Committee what we have affectionately called the 'not suitable for the purpose' letter.

28th October 1967-Tom's letter to the Committee saying, 'Sorry we're not suitable nor the Committee able to accept our entry provisionally, but we will keep trying!'

1st November 1967-Jim had to get into the act in reply to Captain Shaw's earlier correspondence to the effect that the Committee felt that they did not have to prove themselves, but rather that the 'onus was on us.'

14th February 1968-Tom's letter to the Committee explaining why 'the boat capsized'. (More about that later). It sure was a black day in Calcutta when we had to write this one!

20th February 1968-The final 'not suitable' letter from Captain Shaw.

By then we hardly knew where to turn or what to do. In all fairness to the Race Committee, we understood their position in our particular case and knew exactly that they had a responsibility to the sponsor of the race, The Observer, as well as to themselves. In spite of the great disappointment, the spirit of Project 68 was undaunted and we read his letter with much interest and enjoyed the superb British humor and frankness.

'I note that you are taking steps to enable the crew to right the vessel when it has capsized, but my Committee are more interested in any steps you may take to stop the capsizing in the first place. We are still of the opinion that to race along at 25 knots in between periodically capsizing is not a proper way to cross the Atlantic' (we were in full agreement) 'nor could the yacht be considered suitable within the meaning of our rules'.

Finally it dawned on me that this was really a rather emphatic 'no'. Did the word 'nor' and the word 'suitable' really mean what they meant? After a lengthy conference, the project team eventually came to the conclusion that, yes, those two words meant we were not to show up.

Well we were naive enough or stubborn enough not to take 'no', for an answer. We had confidence in *Cheers* even if the Race Committee had not. We had corrected the problem of capsizing, thanks to Dick's great ingenuity, so it was at this moment that we said, 'Forget about shipping the boat--she'll have to be sailed to England. We must prove the point that she is sea-worthy and she does have suitable accommodation for a single-hander, even if our Tom is a most unique single-hander'.

30th March 1968-Tom jots a note to Captain Shaw to say that we were coming!

But I am running ahead too fast.

Chapter two

Work to be done

When there is work to be done, time seems to pass by so very quickly. We were now into late September and I think Dick and Tom were warmly pleased with the progress that had been made. Perhaps the gods were with us at this particular moment.

The progress that had been made on the boat was due in very large measure to Wally Galloway who was sincerely interested on our behalf, as well as the fact that a young man from England had come sailing into Christiansted harbour in his very small trimaran, *Klis,* early in September. His name was Bernard Rhodes and he had designed and built his own boat and the proof of his success was a record-breaking Transatlantic crossing.

Designers and builders certainly seem to attract each other and Bernard found his way to Dick's office and shortly after to the workshop.

As for Dick himself, well throughout the construction period he found himself working not only as a day labourer on the boat, but also as a Master in ordering materials and equipment, and hound-dogging the various companies which had not fulfilled our requests. He also had to run his flourishing charter business of Sea Rovers Inc. and so as well was Mr. Executive.

For several months now the entire team had been assigned the job of deciding upon a name for the boat. We were perhaps only a month away from the launching date and we wanted to have her christened rather than rolling her into the surf just known as 'the boat'. Then one day in October, Pat, Dick Newick and I were seated quietly in one of our favourite late afternoon haunts--The Old Quarter--having a drink to celebrate a day when things had gone especially well. It was at this executive meeting, as we looked out over the serene and quaint harbour of Christiansted, that

Project Cheers

we unanimously hit upon the name for our boat. Perhaps it came in on a fresh Caribbean breeze.

Cheers would be her name. Why *Cheers* ? Well, it may not be widely known but Tom Follett has a great fondness for the British way of life and especially for the manner of toasting. For years, when signing off, in letter after letter, Tom had done so by jotting, '*Cheers* , Follett'. An immediate meeting of the minds on the name was most reassuring.

Several weeks later, Pris Follett wrote to me showing great enthusiasm for the name, and asking how we ever thought of it. It was great fun telling her the story and she was quite surprised.

During this time, incidentally, Tom was busying himself in Coconut Grove, Miami, (when he wasn't delivering a yacht somewhere, that is) by studying his charts, his diet and physical requirements and running last minute errands for Dick to get special pieces of equipment that were unobtainable in the islands.

One such piece of gear, though, called for special tooling and craftsmanship, as well as a little improvisation and this was the steering gear. Though we do seem to lack the technical knowledge for unique yachting gear in Denver, Colorado I was confident that we had a company which could perform this task most admirably: I called on the assistance of George Zimmerman, a young engineer at the firm of William G. Zimmerman Architectural Metals Inc., who was a close friend of mine.

With detailed drawings furnished by Dick Newick I went off, a layman to speak with professionals. It wasn't long after our first greeting that George recognised that Jim Morris knew very little about what he needed, so direct contact was made with Dick on St Croix.

Well to cut a long story short, George assured me the job could be done and would be ready by a specific date. I took it upon myself to organise the delivery of a sizeable crate by air so that it would arrive in St Croix twelve hours later! Would you believe – 12 days later it was delivered! This was perhaps the first time that I really had to play an organising role in a well organised set up and it would certainly appear I fumbled the ball. Anyway this is just one little example of the difficulties we ran into over the delivery of certain items that were so important to *Cheers'* construction.

Would you believe that one reason why we didn't launch in November, but rather in mid-December, was the fact that we lost so much time in our workshop because the electrical power on the island always seemed to fail us when the sanders and the lathes were most needed?

We talk about Project 68 being Newick, Follett, and Morris, but there were many other people equally dedicated to every aspect of our endeavours. Dick was in touch, from time to time, with H. G. (Blondie) Hasler from Southampton, England. We had contacted him, earlier and he had been very helpful in answering various questions of Dick's. Unfortunately he felt later that his 'unofficial' but close relationship with the Race Committee prevented him from truly ending up as a project consultant. Anyway we were all very proud eventually to meet Blondie in England and before we left we felt we had gained a sincere new friend.

No one participated more eagerly and more enthusiastically than Major Ian Major of St Thomas. Whenever we had to talk to somebody who knew what they were talking about, who could be critical but yet constructive and most always come up with the right answer, we would call on Ian. Ian and his wife Cynthia were so much part of the team that they went to England to help us with the last minute arrangements. They were a driving spirit.

Then there was Dave Dana of St Thomas, a naval architect, who was of tremendous help and encouragement throughout. He assisted Dick so many times in coming up with the right formula for the proper strain or stress or saw to it that a piece of hardware was delivered on time. It seems that Dave was always the one who said it could be done and there must be a way--and there was!

Nor will any member of the project team forget the great contribution to our well being made by Dick Eames of St Croix, another fine individual with many sea-going experiences and yachts of his own to his credit. It was Dick who made available to the project team while in England his 70-ft yacht, *Andiamo*. He was a very gracious host.

Finally throughout the entire operation of Project 68 we had the good fortune to have a very great friend, the renowned photographer, Fritz Henle, record the significant aspects and events of *Cheers* and her accomplishments.

So much thought had been given to the design and construction that, embarrassingly enough in early October it dawned on the project team that little or no thought had been given to our engine-that is the sails. It's strange that in this day of sophisticated advertising and the medias corporations use to persuade the general public to use their product, that when we started looking for sailmakers, the response in each case after we had detailed the use for the sails, was that no one was interested in our problem. We knew how to build a boat but admittedly we didn't know all the ramifications of making sails and we were seeking help. Even those renowned sailmakers throughout the world that advertise, 'let us help you with your problem' found our problem not their problem and almost suggested rudeness in their response.

Dave Dana came up with the answer and he was not wrong. He put us in touch with a very capable and enthusiastic sailmaker called Manfred Dietrich. He literally put us back in business within 24 hours. It was his sails, mainsail and various jibs which took *Cheers* to England in record time. Admittedly, perhaps more out of friendship than of need, we had lighter weight sails cut in England for the mainsails, but to this very day, the genoa, No. I jib and the No.2 are perfect, truly the pulling power for *Cheers* and held up extremely well from the day we left St Croix on 30th March 1968 to our return to Christiansted in late July of 1968, some 10,000 miles later.

One thing that had been decided while in St Croix was that we should try to obtain life insurance for Tom. Tom objected to this but we outvoted him and at last sold him the idea by pointing out that the benefit was not for him but for Pris.

Getting life insurance was difficult! The insurance companies' questions made our correspondence with the Race Committee seem as though there was no difference of opinion at all. $100,000 is what we asked for and finally got, but at such a premium that, had the project payed me, I would have considered taking the risk. Still, if the insurance company didn't turn us down, how possibly could the Race Committee?

Dick was confident that the launching would be in the first week or so of December. However he wouldn't give a specific date, understandably. This was sad because I wanted to have some engraving done on some pewter mugs which would be used to toast *Cheers* as she rolled into the surf. To this day the mugs merely recite December 1967. At last a wire from Dick arrived in Denver: 'Tom here. *Cheers* coming along nicely for Tuesday launching. See you soon. *Cheers*, Newick.' Tuesday was the 12th of December.

Sadly Pris Follett was not able to be there. Tootie and I arrived on the 8th to help with the last minute arrangements. For one who is a true neophyte in the business of being part of a sailing campaign, the launching held tremendous excitement and anticipation --- I am surprised there wasn't a coronary involved.

It was a perfect Caribbean day. I think there must have been 150 or 200 friends and onlookers standing around. Somewhat contrary to Caribbean practice, *Cheers* was not built right on the shoreline, and consequently she had to be trailered for a quarter of a mile or so down to the water's edge. In the crowd I am sure there were many who, months ago, had said to themselves or friends off in quiet places, 'Newick is at it again. He has some harebrained idea that he can build a boat like no other boat in the world and would you believe that in addition to that he thinks she will be able to sail backwards and forwards?' However; *Cheers* looked magnificent, a very formidable craft. It seemed certain that we had a potential winner on our hands. Ian Major and Dave Dana had flown from St Thomas for the occasion.

We had read of the launchings of other contenders in the race. These all appeared to be so formal and staid: the usual speeches, all the code flag flying, the slipways greased, or the crane operator anxiously awaiting the signal to 'let her go'. We had no intention of being so formal but rather we had the mere desire in the spirit of friendship, and continual jocularity to see that *Cheers* was properly sent on her way. She was painted a bright canary yellow and the local inhabitants had affectionately dubbed her the 'banana split'. When it came to breaking a champagne bottle on her bow, we had a problem. We had either four bows or four sterns or a minimum of two bows and two sterns, depending on which way *Cheers* was going at any particular time. Tootie was asked to christen her and did so with great gusto, offering her good wishes to the boat and her crew -- 'I christen thee *Cheers*. May God bless her and the man at the helm'. *Cheers* was rolled, if not somewhat lifted, gracefully into the surf and she was afloat. The toasting mugs came in handy and, thanks to Pat Newick, no one lacked a good days portion of champagne. *Cheers* was towed from the launching site by Dick's power boat *Providencia* and for the first time the three of us went sailing.

By nightfall of the 12th of December, all who had participated in the days events knew very well that something very significant had taken

Project Cheers

place. The project team convened for dinner as the final event for the day and the occasion called for 'Popping the cork' on the very generous and thoughtful gift from Cynthia Major to *Cheers*. It was with her greeting that the day finally ended: 'To *Cheers*, may she have a safe passage--a long life--happy and safe sailing---Dear Jim, Dick and Tom, wish I were there to give her an extra blessing, but Ian has left me with all of the things he does not want to do. Nevertheless my thoughts and blessings and wishes are with you all and those who sail in her. Affectionately, Cynthia.'

1. *Cheers* under construction: Bernard Rhodes stands by one of the incredibly slim hulls. *Photo Newick*
2. *Cheers'* aka being laminated. Spruce glued with resourcinal glue. *Photo Newick*

3. *Cheers* under construction, showing the 12mm ply bulkheads bracketing the centerboard trunk, mast, and 'aka'. Note the 6 laminations in the 'aka' (left) *Photo Newick*.
4. Wallford Galloway, who did most of the building. Photo Fritz Henle

Chapter three

Final arrangements

The excitement and fun of the launching had now passed. Tom and I remained in St Croix for a few more days to get our first impression of the way the boat was handling.

Immediate consideration was given to lengthening the booms and to the question of what type of gooseneck fitting we should have. Was it possible to have roller reefing? Perhaps we should consider increasing the size of the spray rails on the bow-sterns. What type of arrangement were we to have for the cockpit? How would we make the cockpit at least spray-tight, if not watertight? How about navigation lights and where would they be located? What about the electrical power? We knew we needed a navigation table and a bunk, but the exact location still had to be decided upon. A lot of thought was given to the size of the booms --- perhaps they were too heavy and clumsy---perhaps a sprit arrangement, eliminating the booms, would solve our problems.

Dick found himself faced with a multitude of questions. Tom and I were good at raising questions---but it fell on Dick's shoulders to come up with the answers.

With Christmas at hand we all soon dispersed to our respective homes leaving Dick with all the problems. No gear or equipment had been placed on board *Cheers* for the sole reason that we wanted to make sure that wherever we put a winch or a cleat, it would only need to be placed once and not changed. Thus it was well into January before these major items were finalised so that Tom could use them to best advantage.

Shortly after the New Year I met Tom in Miami with a view to buying all the extra items that he needed. Shopping for *Cheers* was like Christmas all over again---charts, map cases, cushions, nuts, bolts, blocks, flashlight batteries, cooking stove, navigation lights, all fell into the category of 'get it now as we might not find it in St Croix'.

One article that we really couldn't find was a one man life raft. It was not until a few days before the race that we actually acquired one. Being

Project Cheers

somewhat of a landlubber I was more concerned about this than anyone else. Tom thought it superfluous and sailed to England without one. If it had not been a must in the regulations he would probably have come back without one too.

Cheers was a boat that to the eye was most modern but as far as the application of sailing principles, equipment and construction were concerned, she was so simple that she might even be related to the Stone Age.

With our Christmas shopping done for *Cheers*, we flew to St Croix with the sole purpose in mind that in the next three or four weeks Tom and Dick would prepare her for her first long sea-going voyage. The purpose for the lengthy trip was not only to test *Cheers* but for Tom to come back and make additional suggestions for alterations, see whether or not his stores list was adequate, and very definitely try to hunt down some of the gremlins that we were sure were still aboard. It was not long after we arrived in St Croix that I think it is fair to say that the entire project team was perhaps at its lowest ebb as far as being able to appraise what needed to be done and to accomplish the many tasks that lay ahead.

In our absence Dick had made some very fine and worthwhile decisions and was continuing to 'experiment' with various ideas. For a while all of us were in the experimenting mood, but it dawned on us somewhere late in January that we could no longer afford to experiment. Decisions had to be made, alterations had to be firmed up, and we had to get on with the task---right or wrong. It was at a very early morning meeting on the 20th January that almost simultaneously the triumvirate said: 'No longer can we experiment. Whatever changes we now make will have to be final. Questions are no longer the name of the game but answers instead.'

It was like a dark cloud which had hung over our heads for some time was being completely evaporated or blown away. The sun once again shone; our objectives were very clear; and for sure time was of the essence. We finalised our thoughts regarding roller-reefing. We would have none -- reef points instead. *Cheers* would be a boat that to the eye would be most modern---way out I'm sure in some other people's eyes.

Dick had already reduced the weight and size of each mast by 25 lbs. We were no longer thinking about using a sprit type of arrangement, but of reverting to the old-fashioned gaff jaw for the boom to pivot round the mast. We knew that *Cheers* could carry more sail area and so we increased the length of each boom by splicing in an additional 18 in.

All hands seemed to be eager and all bodies willing. What needed to be done was done almost overnight. To me it appeared that our accomplishments, in such a short period of time, could almost be classified as the Eighth Wonder of the World. Things were really buzzing and there seemed to be a new elation exuding from the whole project team. Manfred, the sailmaker, was finalising and cutting the new sails and it wasn't long before Tom was ready to set sail for the first lengthy voyage. It was necessary for me to return to Denver before Tom's anticipated return and I regretted not having the opportunity of seeing him come back.

If there was ever a time in the life of the project when I began to feel the pressure bearing down, I think it was during the last three weeks of January 1968. We knew by then that we would have to sail *Cheers* to England and consequently the end of March was all too near. However, flying back to Denver at maybe 39,000 ft, I found myself choked with emotion for I knew that we still had much to do and little time to do it in, but deep down I was very confident the end would be satisfactory to all.

Yet for some strange reason I had a feeling of foreboding, leaving St Croix while Tom was still at sea on his first major voyage in *Cheers* and with the outcome still undecided.

On Thursday morning 8th February the feeling of foreboding was to take on a real meaning when Dick called and said, 'Tom is OK, but *Cheers* has capsized in the Caribbean.'

What a feeling of helplessness swept over me---and yet really what could I have done to help, being in Denver and receiving news that, in essence, almost meant that we would have to 'scrub' Project 68? If we were to maintain our philosophy of reporting everything to the Royal Western, how could we now expect them to possibly allow us to enter the Race?

At that moment of greatest discouragement it seemed that Dick pulled the hardest at the bootstraps and brought me to the realisation that all was not lost. He had spoken to Tom by phone who by then had been safely picked up and taken to an island. He had de-briefed Tom to the point that together they had guessed perhaps what had caused *Cheers* to capsize and Dick was not to be denied his entry of *Cheers* in the Race by virtue of this capsize. As it was reported to me, before Tom even returned

Project Cheers

to St Croix, Dick had a solution on the drawing board. It was the right solution---a sponson or blister on the weatherhull so constructed as should a capsize 'aback' ever occur again, the boat would have so much buoyancy that with the help of wind and sea, or just the weight of the crew himself, it could be righted.

To this day I am confident that because of Dick's innovation, *Cheers* is the only ocean-going multi-hull in the world that, if capsized, can be righted by one man. Tom returned to St Croix with *Cheers* and in lengthy consultation with Dick, agreed to his plans and so it truly was a good day in Denver as well as in St Croix when I received the wire 'Stability increased greatly in harbour test---' Admittedly the wire went on to say: 'But self-righting uncertain. Awaiting wind for sea-going test. *Cheers*, Newick.'

My files indicate, needless to say, that there was much correspondence between Newick, Follett and Morris in the next few weeks, all of which gave new hope as to the success of Dick's innovation and *Cheers* readiness to sail to England. Things were now back in what appeared to be equilibrium. I know to this day that Dick and Tom are both of the opinion that the blister really does little for *Cheers*, structurally or in appearance, only adds weight.

My, how the month of February passed us by. We only had 30 days to get ready for the race although we knew that the official start was 1st June. Our schedule had called for *Cheers* to leave St Croix no later than the last day of March. If her passage was successful we expected to have little or nothing to do in the way of refitting her in England. As all the other participants reached the starting line on 1st June so, in effect, we reached our starting line on Sunday 31st March 1968.

The Morris family arrived in St Croix for the Spring vacation on 15th March. Tom was expected on the 25th. To this very day I know of no man who is more casual yet more accomplished in organising himself and those about him than Tom Follett, for it was only to be six days after his arrival that, as he said, he would 'nip over to England'!

During the last two weeks of March the organisation for moving the project team to England was done. Before we had ever started it was mutually agreed that Dick and Pat, Tom and Pris, Tootie and I would be in Plymouth, come Hell or highwater, for the start of the race. By now we had had several meetings with Ian Major and Dick Eames about our plans for the trip to England.

Hank and Annie, two delightful and willing people, left for England on 30th March so as to make sure our home away from home, *Adiamo*, would be ready for our invasion. Dick Eames was to leave in the middle of April, Ian and Cynthia Major at approximately the same time. Pris Follett, Dick Newick, Tootie and Jim Morris would all leave their respective homes to fly to London on Friday, 3rd May. Pat Newick was to follow in our footsteps on 15th May.

All this needed quite some arranging and there was a time when the only thing we were really sure of was Tom's transportation to England, as we just had to head him eastwards in *Cheers* and say, 'Find England'. Hopefully he would be there on our arrival.

Project Cheers

Chapter Four

An anxious wait

It wasn't until the first week in April that we were able to firm up our lodging arrangements in Newport, Rhode Island. We had received many suggestions from friends as to where we should stay, but delving into them only led us to believe that our friends have very expensive tastes.

The City of Newport has a magnificent Chamber of Commerce and after we had dropped them a note detailing our requirements, they sent back several suggestions, one of which fitted our group just perfectly. After several phone calls and an advance deposit, our home from home in Newport became Ocean Vista on Chastellux Avenue, only a block or so away from the Ida Lewis Yacht Club, the official club for finishing the race, an extremely easy walk as it was all downhill---a slightly weary challenge at the end of the day, meandering back up the hill.

Time was passing on and the anticipated departure of *Cheers* to England was at hand. We probably held more meetings of the project team in these last few days than all the times previous with the last minute details of not only preparing *Cheers* but also looking after the necessary but very bothersome details of making sure that Tom had sufficient money for expenses upon his arrival in England---we didn't think he'd be too big a spender on the way over! There was the last minute detail of issuing a bill of sale from Sea Rovers, Inc., the great decision of whether we should use the cistern water from our home or the well water at the Newicks for Tom's supply of H_2O---all ten gallons of it. Tom, in his own inimitable way, asked if I would not come along with him to purchase the final stores for the trip. I wasn't needed for suggestions, but rather to push the buggy through the supermarket.

You could just feel the tempo pick up throughout not only the project team, but those who had so eagerly participated in '*Cheers*' construction through Sea Rovers, Inc. The multitude of friends which Dick and Pat Newick had on the island of St Croix were eagerly checking in daily to make sure what day we had picked for the departure. 'It will probably be Sunday morning, 31st March', they were told.

It was during this time that Dick and Tom decided that *Cheers* would benefit from the addition to each of the bow-sterns what we called, for want of a better name, anti-diving planes. They were nothing spectacular, just pieces of aluminium bolted securely onto the stem so as to give additional lift to the bows whenever *Cheers* decided to dive rather than skim gracefully through or leap over an unexpected sizeable wave. These were personally designed, cut and mounted by Dick.

Tom took off for a day or two's sail and came back to St Croix proclaiming that he was satisfied that *Cheers* was ready to sail to England. I am sure that had *Cheers* herself been capable of expressing any sentiments she would have said that she was ready, too, to take Tom across the pond. Finally we tried hard to ensure that before *Cheers* left all those who had taken an active part in any way would enjoy a sail.

On Saturday evening, 30th March, we decided to have, as so often in the past, a family get-together. Needless to say Tom was the object of our attentions, but just the same he entertained us by strumming on his guitar, always responding to our requests for our favourite songs.

'Early to bed and early to rise, makes a man healthy, wealthy and wise' did not apply to us one bit, for way into the small hours we continually recalled every aspect of the project. How I wished I had been able to tape a recording of the evening's events.

Sunday morning, 31st March, was one for early rising and I wonder why? Tootie's mother was determined that Tom should not sail without a few healthy, well-balanced roast beef sandwiches in hand. I doubt if any sandwiches were made with more loving care.

Rain, rain, rain---this certainly was not the day to send Tom off to England, but it was still early morn and in the Caribbean you can almost definitely count on the sky clearing and the sun shining by 10 a.m. As though we had ordered the weather ourselves the sun shone brightly by 9 a.m., the faces of all concerned were wreathed in smiles and no-one needed to tell us that we had finally reached our starting line and were on time.

Our plans called for towing Tom and *Cheers* out of the harbour with *Providencia*, Dick's motor launch. We had invited a host of friends and we all boarded *Providencia*, threw *Cheers* the towline and in a matter of minutes Project 68 was on its way to England. The inquisitive, as well as close friends of the Newicks, and I am sure, even some sceptics, lined the shore and each in his individual way wished Tom well. It was now 10 a.m. and a bell high in a steeple was ringing most noticeably. It, too, seemed to say 'God speed'. There was commotion, no confusion, but rather a stillness which even the diesel engine in *Providencia* could not disturb. Each person on the launch was praying for Tom's safety and a speedy voyage, but those close to the project could not, I am sure, help but recall that not so long before we had sent Tom off on a lengthy voyage and that *Cheers* had capsized!

To all outward appearances Tom was his usual collected, cool-as-a-cucumber self---just another trip. The sails were hoisted, the last minute adjustments were made, the towline hauled in and a moment of history was made. *Cheers* and Follett were once again on their own. We tried in *Providencia* to keep up with Tom, but *Cheers* was like a racehorse coming out of the starting gate and as much as said, 'Don't bother me, I've got to get to a race.'

We had some idea of Tom's route for he had confided in us that there were two alternatives. He might either head north, perhaps stopping over in Bermuda for a few days before going on to England, or, if the winds were favourable avoid Bermuda altogether and make straight for England.

The run back to Christiansted harbour only took a matter of minutes and the silence was almost deafening. Tootie turned to me and with a very sincere embrace and tears of joy whispered, 'You've done it'. There was no question in my mind that she affectionately meant the you for Dick and Tom as well as me.

When flying home 40 minutes later we had only gained altitude of about 10,000 ft when over the loudspeaker in the cabin a very interested navigating officer informed us that *Cheers*, the Virgin Island's entry in the Single-Handed Transatlantic Race of 1968 had been spotted off our starboard quarter and was moving out smartly. Tom at this time was half-way across to St Thomas. What a nice way to return to Denver, knowing the beginning was so perfect.

I am no different from the rest of us and I must confess that I have never experienced a more difficult time than the ensuing period of waiting. If anything should ever deter me from joining another Newick,

Project Cheers

Follett, Morris project team, it would be the doubt as to whether I could really go through the anxiety of waiting, waiting, waiting, not knowing, only hoping and praying and guessing that no news was good news. To me it was utter Hell. If the truth were known even salty Newick, highly experienced in the ways of the sea, almost philosophic in his approach to her severity as well as her gentleness, had to admit to some concern and apprehension.

On my return home that very evening I called Pris and as best I could relayed the happenings of the past two weeks, desperately trying to assure her that all was well and we were most confident.

Then one day I received in the mail from Dick Newick a newspaper clipping relating to Eric Tabarly and *Pen Duick IV*. Somewhere amid the verbiage was a sentence which could so easily have been left out, but thank goodness, had been left in. It merely said that in the very near future final registration of all the anticipated entrants would have to be received by the Royal Western Yacht Club of England, the closing date being 1st May. I was amazed for we had been under the impression that final registration had to be done by 15th May! It hit me like a thunderbolt that even if we got to England, we technically might not be acceptable by virtue of the fact that we had not registered on time. It wasn't that we hadn't tried; it was just that the Race Committee earlier in the game had returned our money. I broke into a cold sweat---what should we do now?

Once again we reverted to the phone and I called Ian Major in Chobham, England. I explained the situation to him and he agreed that something had to be done immediately. This was on Good Friday, 12th April. Ian said that he would cable me with his results and so a waiting game within a waiting game immediately took place. We thought we might have his reply by Easter Sunday, but it was not until Monday morning that a very excited Western Union boy delivered the telegram which read as follows, 'Have good news stop After excellent briefing by Hasler I talked Odling-Smee Chairman SHTR Committee stop He will accept *Cheers* as provisional entry stop Am sending entry form and fee on behalf Tom stop On arrival Plymouth Odling-Smee will personally inspect *Cheers* and give final decision Regard Ian.'

Hallelujah.

Prior to Tom's departure we had had a meeting with Ian Major and Dick Eames and laid the strategy for Tom's arrival in England. Originally we had thought perhaps he should sail right into Plymouth, drop his hook and advise them that he was there. This might have been OK if at the time of the meeting we had known of a provisional acceptance, but we did not. In fact, at that particular moment we had been asked in so many words not to come. In every decision that we made regarding *Cheers* and her acceptance into the race it was our paramount concern not to give the Race Committee the impression that we were forcing our way or, should our crossing from St Croix to England be successful, that we would make them accept us.

We had read enough about, perhaps even experienced, the 'ugly American' and felt that come Hell or high water, the success or failure of Project 68 would never reflect this attitude. As naive as it may sound, we promised ourselves that whatever decision the Race Committee made about our entry it would be accepted graciously and with full realisation that the Royal Western had the final say. Admittedly we would be disappointed if rejected and would have to return to the United States.

We would then sail the Atlantic and just happen to be sailing for Newport. However, I assure you most sincerely, we had decided not to leave Plymouth on 1st June, but rather wait in good taste and head for Newport after the official start. We were confident, however, that if *Cheers* arrived in England for the purpose of entering the race, we could not help but be an object of interest as well as concern to those in the world of yachting.

For this reason it was decided it would perhaps be better to hide away for as long a period of time prior to the race as possible, hoping not to be the centre of anyone's attention. Also there was the matter of being practical. If she got to England *Cheers* would probably need quite a bit in the way of refurbishing. So, at the suggestion of Dick Eames we made our immediate destination Gosport, more particularly, Camper and Nicholsons Ltd., the shipyard where *Andiamo* was being fitted out.

The project team was so emphatic in their feeling about not wanting to pressure or influence the Race Committee's final decision by public opinion that we actually laid down a rule that only Follett, Newick or Morris would speak to the press, radio or TV on behalf of the project. We were, admittedly, gun-shy, when it came to publicity and it was at the suggestion of Ian Major that we put together a public relations kit, consisting of a sheet of facts about *Cheers* and her team, together with a photograph. Five hundred were produced and we returned to Newport with very few in hand.

It was also decided that before we left Gosport to sail to Plymouth to present ourselves to the Race Committee we would have an independent survey made of the boat. In essence what we were trying to do was to arrive in Plymouth ready in every respect and ready to offer the Race Committee an outside, unbiased survey of condition and readiness. Camper and Nicholsons was not only a hideaway but also gave us the opportunity of having any alterations, adjustments and repairs made to *Cheers* that were needed by one of the best boat yards in England.

My, how I wish I had the ability to translate into words the feelings of those days of waiting from 31st March to 28th April. Tom had expected to make England in about 21 days, so in reality, for 21 days or thereabouts, we had no anxiety or concern. But on the stroke of midnight on the 21st day, with no word from Tom, a feeling akin to nausea came over me.

'Why, Tootie, have we not heard from Tom?'

On the 23rd day I was in a directors meeting away from my home and it was then that Tootie transferred a call from England to me. It was Hank Chamberlain calling from Gosport, merely a call of friendship and concern that *Cheers* had not arrived. He and Ian Major had concluded that since the weather, according to their reports was not in Tom's favour, they now had to re-evaluate his progress, and his ETA they figured to be approximately the 27th or 28th April.

This phone call laid my concern to rest, if only for a matter of days. I think only once during this time did I talk to Dick in St Croix. Outwardly he was most reassuring and I wonder if, in addition to his accomplishments in design and sailing, he is not a damned good actor.

It was but a few days before Pris Follett, the Morrises and Dick Newick would be heading for England and what a horrible feeling it was to think we might leave the United States not knowing whether Tom had reached the mother country. If he had not arrived before we left what a flight that would be.

Don't ask me why I never left the house on 29th April---don't ever tell me that intuition is not one of the great motivating forces of man. At 11.15 a.m., Rocky Moutain Standard Time, the phone rang. Tootie answered it. Never will I forget that shriek that Tootie let out when she said,

'Jim, it's England---Tom!'

'Hello, Morris here.'
'Follett here.'
And how silly, I said,
'Where?'
'Where did you expect?'
'I don't know Tommy, but just tell me you're in England.'

For days I had written questions on scrap paper of things to ask Tom when he called. What a useless therapy that was for nary a question did I ask. On hanging up the receiver I gave thanks, wept for joy and knew immediately that others must participate in this moment. A phone call to Pris in Miami was true happiness. A call to Dick in St Croix found he was not there, but on his way to the airport, flying to meet us in New York. Pat Newick received the good news, the word of the day, and said that if I would stop talking, she thought she could get the news to Dick before he boarded his plane for New York.

She was successful for, just before the hatch closed, the airline representative came bounding up the stairs, paging Mr. Newick, and handed him the note---'Boat *Cheers* arrived in England. Everything fine.'

All of us would now be flying to England with light hearts, determined spirit, and thankfulness.

Project Cheers

Chapter five

Gosport and Plymouth

It was very difficult to imagine and yet so pleasing to know that Project 68 was still on schedule. Tom had arrived in England. Pris Follett, Dick Newick and the Morrises had all met as planned at the International Hotel in New York on the evening of 2nd May so as to catch a flight to England the next morning. The excitement was almost more than most of us could take. It was as though we were in our own little world, caring very little about those around us, but bubbling with enthusiasm as we winged our way across the Atlantic, looking down at the sea only as a matter of interest rather than concern as to whether or not we would have to spot Tom.

As the plane touched down, I am sure we were all wondering just who would be on hand to meet us. I knew that my assignment was to look for the man in a long grey coat from the Savoy, for Dick Eames had arranged that this man would see that we got through customs and on our way to the hotel. As we came into the main airport building our questions were answered, for there was the whole group, the vanguard of the project team, all looking up as we descended the escalator. Not to be taken lightly or forgotten was the thoughtful telegram Tom had in his hand from Captain Shaw which set the tone for our arrival in England: 'Congratulations on splendid voyage. Shaw, Royal Western.'

Thanks to Dick Eames attention to detail we had chauffer-driven cars at our disposal all Saturday and we took advantage of the leisure time to go sightseeing and to make a few purchases for *Cheers*. Sunday morning when we congregated in the Eames' suite at the Savoy was the first opportunity we had to read about *Cheers* as noted by a reporter in the *Observer*. No-one took offense at the remark that *Cheers* resembled a 'Child's yellow cellulose bath toy'.

We understood that some of the contestants still had to make their 500 mile qualifying voyage and it was hard for us to fathom how, when so close to the start, there could be so many who still had to sail off and

Project Cheers

return. If this was the case Project 68 was not only on schedule, but qualifying run under his belt---a few miles in excess of that necessary. His trip from St Croix to Gosport , covered 4,200 single-handed miles, about 1,000 miles in excess of what it would take him to Newport.

Upon our arrival at Camper & Nicholsons Ltd., Gosport, it was such a surprise to see *Cheers* hauled up in the shipyards' general parking area, yet there she sat, almost proclaiming, 'You're late, I beat you. Don't I look great?' Believe it or not it was at this very moment that Pris Follett saw *Cheers* for the very first time. Whatever she thought of her, we all knew that *Cheers* had so far lived up to all our expectations. She had made a historic passage, she had brought Tom safely to England and she looked in as perfect condition as the day she left the islands.

Tom and Pris used the next two weeks in Gosport to go off on several two day jaunts round the countryside visiting old friends and acquaintances of years past. Dick Newick and the Morrises stayed very close to the ship-yard, Dick leaving only to go to London when Pat arrived from the States on 15th May. Dick Eames was in and out for he had many things to do and catch up on before taking *Andiamo* to Plymouth. He had to plan his cruising for the entire summer and early fall in Scandinavian waters. In spite of all he had to do, though, he always had time to direct us to the right person to get jobs done on *Cheers*.

Life to say the least was most pleasant in these very comfortable surroundings. After we somewhat settled down to a normal daily routine it dawned on us that a few things had to be accomplished on *Cheers* prior to our departure on 18th May. There was plenty of time for little had to be done, but perhaps there wasn't that much time if we sat on our hands when the sun was shining. Now was the time to do the work.

Another project meeting decided what needed to be done on *Cheers*. A few areas on her decks were to be painted with non-slip paint. The mast-coats needed to be replaced to prevent the rather noticeable amount of seepage into the cockpit from the spray and breaking waves. Though we were still awaiting our official acceptance we had been issued a number and 41 had to be painted on the side of the sponson as well as on the deck area of the outrigger. We decided it would not hurt to have the bottom repainted, though, in all honesty, it was not absolutely necessary.

Tom had registered his desire to have new main sails cut and he visited Bunty King, at Hood Sailmakers Ltd., Lymington. Our last minute request for new sails from the Hood loft and their acceptance of the order to our time schedule was truly a concession for they were in the midst of their late spring jam-up. The sails were made and delivered on time and were extremely satisfactory. Tom was pleased.

A very small area of one of our dagger boards needed fiber-glassing --- a must. Tom also wanted the area of each of the anti-diving planes increased and strengthened. The cutting of new sails and this last request were perhaps the two most urgent things that we had to get done before leaving for the States.

With Hank Chamberlain's help, direction and side introductions to individuals who would actually do the work, all was accomplished. Admittedly, however, in between rain, fog, sleet, cold wind and actual or pending strikes, there was near the end some real anxiety. It must not be forgotten that we still had not acquired one piece of gear, which was a must so far as the Race Committee was concerned---the one-man life raft. For some reason the life raft problems seemed to bug us from the very beginning of the project. I recall Dick Newick writing to Captain Shaw about this problem. On 9th November 1967 Captain Shaw wrote, 'Dear Mr Newick, Thank you for your letter of 31st October. As regards the life raft, the aviator type would be quite acceptable (I have one at home which is inflated, filled with water, and used as a paddling pool by the grandchildren). Yours sincerely, Terrance W. B. Shaw.'

There was a moment when I thought we might have to encroach on Captain Shaw's good nature and deprive his grandchildren of their pool. Shortly after our arrival at Gosport we made the acquaintance of a gentleman who was having his yacht built by Campers, about-to-be retired Wing Commander Bob Carson. It was through his personal concern for our well-being and his great interest in *Cheers* that we finally had delivered to us at Plymouth a proto-type one-man life raft, developed by Beaufort (air-sea) Equipment Ltd.

As you may recall we had chosen Gosport for several reasons, one of which was to find a place where we could stay out of the public eye. We accomplished our objective in this regard for perhaps a matter of 48 hours, but then the news media fell on top of us. One morning Peter Bale, John Dobson, Elizabeth Hodgson and Bob Fisher of the BBC came aboard *Andiamo*. They were producing a documentary film of a few of the entrants and asked if they could include *Cheers* in some of their footage.

Project Cheers

The film was to be shown on the evening before the start of the race. On the whole we formed a very favourable impression of all British editors, reporters, news commentators and TV representatives.

While in Gosport the project team met each morning to program the day's activities and co-ordinate the efforts of all. *Andiamo* by virtue of, her comfort, spaciousness and accessibility, was the command center and daily news conference room afloat. Interview after interview, footage on footage, we were terribly new to this game of being in the public eye, but I must admit that it was a grand experience and quite fun.

We had a very strong feeling that the Royal Western would not turn us down at this stage of the game, but we had nurtured for many months the philosophy that until acceptance we would leave nothing to chance. With this in mind we decided to obtain from a recognised surveyor of yachts an official survey of *Cheers*, testifying to her readiness and seaworthiness for the Single-Handed Transatlantic Race. We thought that it might help lighten the load the Race Committee had to bear if we could diplomatically present them with a survey. I know we also thought it wouldn't be such a bad idea to know whether some unbiased person felt we were ready.

So we invited Colin Mudie AMRINA to come to Gosport and make an official survey of *Cheers*. His official report and covering correspondence dated 6th May is reproduced here:

Mr Jim Morris,   6 May 1968
Yacht *Cheers* ,
C/O Camper & Nicholsons Ltd.,
Gosport,
Hants.

Dear Mr. Morris,

I enclose two copies of my report and hope that these will be of assistance. Of course, if the Race Committee would like to ring me up to discuss any part of it I will be very happy to help.

I was delighted to see your vessel and must congratulate you all on such an interesting and exciting entry. I think that you may have started a complete new generation of offshore multi-hulls. I think that the windward flotation on the windward hull to make the yacht self-righting is a stroke of genius on the part of Dick Newick.

Please give Tom my best wishes for a fast and successful trip.

Yours sincerely, Colin Mudie

All opinion on the suitability of the 40 foot proa 'Cheers' for single handed sailing, following an inspection of the vessel at Camper & Nicholsons Gosport Yard.

6th May 1968

ORIGIN. This inspection was undertaken at the request of the owner of the yacht, Mr. Jim Morris, who wished to have an independent opinion as to the structural and general design for seaworthiness to put before the organisers of the Third Single Handed Transatlantic Race. The yacht is entered and will be sailed by Mr. Tom Follett.

CONDITION. The proa was hauled out at Camper & Nicholsons Gosport yard. She had recently completed a single handed voyage from the West Indies and apart from the removal of gear and the withdrawing of the twin centreboard/rudders had not been touched. The yacht was said to have experienced a wide range of sea and wind conditions during her passage. The following items were noticed:

1. The foam and reinforced plastics fairings to the stem head washplates were extensively cracked, indicating a fair amount of movement of the plates. These, however, were still securely attached to the stem heads.

2. The wooden deck level washstroke showed minute cracks at the roots in places, indicating that these had also been heavily stressed during the passage.

3. It was just possible to see hair cracks at the roots of the cross beams at their junction to the weather hulls. In addition, the plywood top surface of the deck locker box, part of the same stress system, also showed signs of movement.

This is an extremely modest amount of damage after such a passage. It is understood that the stem head and washplates are to be rebuilt before the race. The other items are negligible.

STRUCTURAL DESIGN. I formed the opinion that the hulls and the structure had been very carefully designed and if anything had an excess of strength at the important structural stress points. The ends of the twin laminated box girders are, for instance, buried in each hull and secured between twin bulkheads. Large foam fairings are used at the roots. In general the level of scantlings employed throughout, appeared to be reasonable as far as they could be ascertained. The buoyancy fairing on the weather side of the weather deck is perhaps a little higher than I would like to see, but I probably strong enough.

The following scantlings were noted or given to me:

- Hulls and deck superstructures ; 3/8" cold moulded African mahogany
- Cross members; 8" sided by 8 1/2" moulded hollow laminated spruce
  1 ½" horizontal walls
  1 7/8" vertical walls ;
- Hull bulkheads   12mm plywood ;
- Weather buoyancy box   6mm plywood ;
- Masts   6 ¾" square to 3 ¾"
  1 ¼" walls tapered to 3/4" walls ;

Hulls, cross members and superstructures all covered in Polypropylene cloth reinforced resin. Cross members specifically two skins 10 ozs. cloth and epoxy resin.

GENERAL DESIGN. In terms of basic buoyancy the craft has been divided up into a number of individual watertight compartments and some of these have been further filled with plastics foam to provide the minimum of, 'crash' buoyancy. In view of the very small amount of metal fittings and absence of ballast keel the buoyancy arrangements would appear to be more than adequate. I understand that a certain amount of flooded tests have been made.

In terms of stability and self righting the designer has provided an ingenious flotation box on the weather side of the weather hull which should greatly aid, if not ensure, righting in the event of a capsize. In addition, the masts are of large section and made to be part of the righting system. In view of the very modest sail area required to drive the vessel it is unlikely that the masts would be ever in danger in the circumstances which would capsize this vessel.

The steering arrangements, using rudders in the centreboards connected to a vertical tiller, are unusual. No sign of damage or wear was visible and no trouble with them was reported. I was told that the proa does not steer easily in narrow waters. The twin centreboards and rudders are interchangeable and therefore equivalent to carrying a spare in case of trouble. The sweep also carried would provide a further safety factor in that it could be used as an emergency steering oar.

The cabin arrangements are adequate for a single hander, although he has little protection working about the decks.

The non-structural joinerwork is in many cases less robust than we are used to seeing but damage here would result more in discomfort for the crew rather than in danger for the yacht. The deck locker tops, for instance, did not appear to have any retaining cords or straps and the entry washboard was without latch.

CONCLUSION. This vessel is, in my opinion, at least as seaworthy as any small multi-hull and, with her self-righting capability, more seaworthy perhaps than most unballasted multi-hulls for a single handed voyage. She also appeared to be built campaigned with great care and attention to detail.

Colin C. Mudie   6th May 1968

We were by no means disappointed on receipt of Colin's survey. Instead we were greatly reassured that in *Cheers* we had an acceptable entry. Would you believe that there was still a sceptic in the crowd--me? Now that we had an official survey of *Cheers* from a very respected and capable surveyor of yachts there was still some doubt running through the team as to what, upon our arrival in Plymouth, the Race Committee might question or ask us to change or add to the boat. If there were some fine suggestions to be made as to alterations by someone who perhaps knew the thinking of the Race Committee, it would be most expedient if we had the work done, while in Gosport rather than in Plymouth where everybody would be jockeying for position with those who could do the work. Who knows, we might be last in line!

Once again we called on Ian Major to trespass on his personal friendship with Lt Col H. G. Hasler so as to have Blondie come down and look *Cheers* over, not with the eye of a surveyor, but more with the eye of a make-believe member of the Race Committee who would make the final decision as to the boats acceptance or refusal.

Blondie's observations, as forwarded to Ian, are reproduced here from his correspondence of 8th May 1968.

Ian Major Esq.,   8th May 1968
Wisteria Cottage,
Broadford,
Chobham,
Surrey.

Many thanks for arranging for me to look at *Cheers* yesterday, and introducing me to her very charming and impressive team.

You asked me to give an imitation of an irritable committee member looking at the boat, so here are a few imaginary critical comments, which may or may not be of any use. As you know, I have no official position in the race organization, and would not want to be quoted as having 'approved' or 'disapproved' anything.

CONDITION

1. The only structural weakness that I noticed was the crack under the 'spoons' at stem and stern. I was doubtful about whether the new and larger spoons wouldn't also try to pull off upwards, unless it were possible to fit a metal strap down the face of the stem.

JOINERY

2. It might be felt that the heads bucket ought to have some sort of hinged or portable seat which held it firm whilst in serious use?

HURRICANE PRECAUTIONS

3. It might be felt that Tom's harness system should enable him to clip himself on before leaving the conning tower, and then get anywhere around the boat without unhooking himself. Possible aids to achieving

this would be jackstays of plastic-covered wire and a harness rope two spring-hooks on it. Hooking on to running ropes may not be regarded as adequate.

4. It might be felt that a stiffened plywood 'hurricane hatch' should be provided to enable the conning tower to be battened down even if the pram hood were lost.

CAPSIZING PRECAUTIONS

5. In order to reinforce the claim of being able to capsize and right the boat with impunity, it might be desirable to show that nothing would be lost or damaged in the process. Perhaps:

(a) Lanyards to prevent the fashion boards of the companionway from getting lost?

(b) All heavy items carried in the cabin to be tied down?

(c) Turnbuttons to hold the lids of the self-draining lockers shut?

Please note that I am not necessarily saying that these things are in fact necessary with this particular boat and crew. I am just trying to forecast the sort of things that might prove to be necessary to keep the committee happy.

Since three reports in the hand would be better than two we did not stop with Messrs Mudie and Hasler, but in addition engaged Mr J. D. Locke, AMRINA. Admittedly Mr. Locke did not make an official survey of the boat, but rather came to Gosport to look at *Cheers* and visit her project team and with no bias render his thoughts for the day. His letter and report of 14th May 1968, follows.

J. R. Morris, Esq.,
U.S. Yacht *Andiamo*,
c/o Camper & Nicholsons Ltd.,
Gosport,
Hants.

Project Cheers

Dear Mr. Morris,

re *Cheers*

Further to our meeting yesterday and the most interesting discussion with you and Mr. Newick I now have pleasure in enclosing my report on this craft.

I hope this will be found to satisfy the Race Committee but if they should require a check of the listed items, when the boat is fully fitted out, I shall be glad to do this for you (preferably before the boat leaves this area).

As a dyed-in-the-wool traditionalist I must admit that the first sight of the boat gave me some qualms but the more I looked at it the more impressed I became and there is no doubt in my mind that she has great possibilities as a single-hander and is a remarkable design concept.

I am satisfied that the hull is a great deal stronger than many of the standard catamarans in use offshore here, of similar size, and should be capable of bearing any normal sailing stresses.

A note of my survey fee is enclosed, as requested.

Yours sincerely, J. D. Locke.

Condition Inspection
40ft Proa *Cheers*

We hereby certify that we have today inspected the yacht *Cheers* of Christiansted, St Croix, U.S. Virgin Islands, lying ashore at Camper & Nicholsons Ltd., Gosport, Hants., rigged and equipped with all essential sailing equipment, except for the items listed hereunder not seen at this time, which T. Follett proposes to carry and use in the Single-handed Atlantic Race.

Insofar as it was possible to inspect them, we consider that the hull, decks, spars, rigging, sails, ground tackle, fittings and sailing equipment appeared to be in good and serviceable condition.

Items considered essential, but not seen at this time include:

Inflatable Liferaft.
Safety Harness.
Lifejacket.

>   Navigational equipment.
>   Sail repair kit.
>   Heavy duty torch.
>   Stores and water stowage.
>
> These items and the remaining equipment listed under Rule 20 will be obtained and put aboard, to bring to a full state of readiness, when the vessel is put afloat.
>
> One item recommended as additional to the above is the provision of a Trysail, suitable for setting on existing spars or loose-footed if necessary, of about 70 sq ft on area and of 10 ozs Terylene.
>
> Wadham Locke Limited, Director.

Well by the time we had received the opinions from the above mentioned an air of confidence was certainly enjoyed by those associated with *Cheers* and though everyone of us wanted to send wires to the States that we would officially be in the race, we bridled our enthusiasm and quietly cherished the anticipated hope of acceptance.

The day of departure from Gosport was getting closer and closer and we finally decided that 18th May it had to be. It was imperative, therefore, that we got our sails from Bunty King on 18th. Bunty did not fail us though his entry into Camper & Nicholsons's yard was like one stealing home plate on a bunt ball, bases loaded, and great confusion at home plate!

Andiamo and *Cheers* were ready to head for Plymonth and there was no reason to wait any longer for 'judgement day'. Let's be on our way -- let's get our answer -- let's see if we would be acceptable to the Race Committee. So on 18th May late afternoon, the project team and its many facets: the Newicks by land, Follett and Morris by sea on *Cheers*, the others on *Andiamo*, took off. There were many farewells before leaving for in the very short period of time, we had all found new friends and hoped this would not be the last time that our paths would cross. Tom, I am quite confident, was making a great concession in inviting me to sail with him to Plymouth. It was an unspoken understanding of many months past that *Cheers* was as a real one-man boat and except for a few hours day sailing, she really was not big enough to accommodate more than one, but Tom in his good natured way said; 'Come on, Jimmy, you have to sail on *Cheers* at least once before we head west.'

Project Cheers

It was well into late afternoon before *Cheers* could honestly be considered as heading for Plymouth. There were BBC television people aboard *Andiamo* as well as on board *Cheers*, taking some last minute footage. God, how I wish the weather had been better. We thought *Andiamo* would cruise along, but before too long, they ran into difficulties and had to be towed into Cowes. *Cheers*, Tom and Jim were on their own. Tom has superbly described the two-man trip in a one-man boat to Plymouth, but I will, for a moment, reflect on a personal observation relative to *Cheers* and her owner. We don't see eye to eye. Now let it be understood right here and now that *Cheers* is a magnificent, exciting and exhilarating boat. I'm confident that at no time would she let you down. The fault comes only with the man at the helm if he's the owner. I remember very vividly, upon renewing my acquaintance with Tootie in Plymouth, that I told her I would never be capable of sailing *Cheers*. She was too much of a boat for me and my experience in ocean sailing was so limited that she absolutely scared me with her speed. I maintain to this day that her designer-builder, as well as her skipper are the only two men I know who will ever be able to sail *Cheers* to her maximum. Others will try -- others have tried, but she is such a lady of the sea (somewhat fickle I'm sure) that she is only happy with either of these two gentlemen at the helm.

Boy was it cold and I mean damned cold! Even Tom Follett says he has never been colder than when we sailed from Gosport to Plymouth. It was about 5.30 in the morning that we arrived offshore of what would be our anchorage for the next eleven days -- Plymouth, England. The seas had calmed; the wind had somewhat abated; and we once again were sailing under our two mainsails. There was a yacht to the lee of us who, by her very maneuvers, one could tell had awakened to the dawn and seen something to her windward which appeared almost unorthodox, but was sailing at a very great speed. The leeward yacht was *Myth of Malham*, sailed by Noel Bevan, coming up hard on the wind to see what this creature was. Actually before we entered the breakwaters at Plymouth, 'old Myth' had passed us by. She knew where she was going --to an anchorage off the Royal Western Yacht Club. We were not sure where the Club was and consequently anchored some distance away. The air was crisp; the sun was bright; yet at this early hour the sun was still very chintzy with her warmth. Tom went below to rest -- in fact to sleep. I somewhat boastfully said I would stand watch, waiting for someone from the Royal Western to come and recognise us, but I immediately fell asleep on deck.

Several hours later and having drifted many hundred yards, we were greeted by the launch from the Royal Western Yacht Club with none other than the Secretary (Sailing) aboard, Captain Terrance W. B. Shaw. I still wonder what Captain Shaw actually thought of *Cheers* and more particularly, the crew, for the only reason we had stopped drifting was due to the fact that our anchor had fouled a cable and could not be lifted aboard. Another Danforth anchor and 60 ft or more of line was offered to Neptune's locker. We were taken into Millbay Docks under the guidance of Captain Shaw. Terrance Shaw is regarded by the members of Project '68 with warm regards and great respect.

Our acceptance in the race was still in abeyance, but most assuredly our arrival in Plymouth had been warmly greeted, *Cheers* accomplishments to date were recognised and there was clearly willingness on the part of the official committee to judge *Cheers* and the skipper on their merits. One could ask for no more.

Project Cheers

Chapter six

Acceptance at last and a good start

By now it was almost noon and the tide was such that we could be towed into the Millbay Docks area, *Cheers* home until the very start of the Race. Shortly after getting squared away it became very noticeable that Tom's ankle had certainly taken a turn for the worse. There had been suggestions by many members of the project team in varying degrees of forcefulness that Tom should have a doctor look at this particular appendage. He was certainly not excited or overly impressed with our behind-the-scenes maneuvering to accomplish this formidable task. He knew how to take care of it and he jolly well would, perhaps better if we would only leave him alone.

Dick and Pat Newick were not expected to check into the Continental Hotel in Plymouth until late Sunday afternoon or perhaps even Monday morning and because of *Andiamo*'s problems at sea, Tom and I weren't quite sure when we would see them next. A generous invitation from Captain Shaw enticed us over to the Royal Western where on our arrival we had the good fun of meeting our early morning competitor, Noel Bevan of the *Myth of Malham*. By late afternoon the Newicks had arrived. We returned to the warmth and friendliness of the Royal Western and there, just off the break-water, the silhouette of *Andiamo* could be seen as the fiery red sun was about to be extinguished. Before nightfall, the project team was once again united.

Cheers upon her arrival at Plymouth was (for all practical purposes) ready to enter the Race. The few things still to be accomplished we had scheduled to do in Plymouth to keep ourselves busy awaiting our acceptance and the start. As far as time spent, these small tasks could have been done in less than a day -- buying an anchor, some chain and line, replacing the halyards, re-stringing the net between the two hulls, taking on a few stores, and finding the one-man life raft which had been posted to our attention.

No problems.

Project Cheers

By now *Andiamo* was securely moored inside the Millbay Docks and *Cheers* was alongside. As each day passed, one could not help but feel the tempo of excitement and exhilaration everywhere. Prominent was the good fellowship amongst the skippers as they checked in. There appeared to be a willingness on the part of many to be as helpful as possible should the entrant have any problems. I'm not quite sure just when it was that we had the opportunity of meeting for the first time Bruce Dalling and his project team. I assure you that upon our meeting and the many visits thereafter, it was quite evident that we were not the only project team in Plymouth who had arrived in an organised fashion.

Time was getting on and our daily circumvention of the Millbay Docks afforded us the opportunity to become acquainted with the many fine skippers and their yachts. Eric Willis, skipper of the 50 ft trimaran, *Coila*, always had a friendly word as we passed by: 'Remember when we get to Newport -- you stay around long enough so I can have a sail on *Cheers*. Unfortunately Eric has yet to have his sail.

Everybody had their problems so 'getting together' with various skippers was almost by happenstance and rarely ever by formal introduction. Our group was very impressed with the *Spirit of Cutty Sark*, a Gallant No 53 class boat.

Much had been said and written in periodicals relative to Bill Howell and his 43 ft ketch catamaran *Golden Cockerel*. He was obviously confident and we of *Cheers* did not underestimate his past achievements or his possible forthcoming accomplishments. Robert Wingate, owner and skipper of *Zeevalk* was a friend of Tom Follett's and though we had asked him to join us aboard *Andiamo* when time permitted, he was just too busy, confronted with so many last minute tasks. Dick Eames had suggested to Mike Richey that he join us alongside *Andiamo* and we felt very distinguished by having *Jester*, designed and sailed by Blondie Hasler in previous races, in our midst. Respectfully she was called the 'old lady' of the '68 Race, having competed in 1960 and 1964. I will never forget the late afternoon of the last week when literally out of the blue came none other than Joan de Kat bounding aboard *Cheers* like a gazelle. He was the absolute picture of enthusiasm and zest for living, the owner and skipper of the 50 ft trimaran *Yaksha*. His English, I assure you, was much better than my French, and as he introduced himself between leaps on the 'trampoline', the net between our hulls, he literally gushed with enthusiasm over *Cheers*. 'Mon Dieu, Mon Dieu, this is the boat I should have in the Race. You are a winner.'

How concerned we all were when we heard that Joan de Kat had abandoned his ship and was lost at sea—and how thankful to the 'Man upstairs' when word was received of his survival. True perhaps—*Yaksha* should not have been an entrant; perhaps others might also fit into this category, but that is not the point. Joan de Kat is an enthusiastic, confident and very determined young man who, I am quite sure, could sell refrigerators to Eskimos and have them buy two in case the first one broke down. God how I wish perhaps there were more like him in this world—most assuredly we couldn't be worse off.

Only nine days before the start and it appeared that *Cheers* would be the only United States entry, or to be more exact, an entrant representing the United States Virgin Islands. *Axel Heyst III*, listed as a United States entrant, had by then informed the Race Committee that she would not participate. It was assumed, too, that Arthur Piver, the owner and skipper of *Stiletto*, an American entry, would not be crossing the starting line, Arthur having been reported lost at sea. The whereabouts of perhaps the only USA entry, Bernie Rodriquez in his 25 ft cutter-rigged trimaran, *Amistad*, was uncertain. Fortunately Bernie arrived, but only after a harrowing 42 day crossing from the states. It was difficult for us who had been in Britain for some time to realize that in nine days he would be homeward bound! He, too, berthed very close to *Cheers*.

I think that here few comments on the general preparedness of the yachts may not come amiss. Perhaps the lack of encouragement from the Race Committee was the stimulant needed in our case to keep us on schedule. Certainly ours was not the only yacht which was ready, but most assuredly the number was small. I am not sure whether or not the yachtsman is the world's greatest procrastinator, but there was a good many of them working diligently, almost in panic, and yet they had had four years in which to prepare—it must be the nature of the beast!

I take my hat off to the truly organized, the dedicated representatives of the Royal Western Yacht Club. As evidence of their attention to detail, they were not only fully involved in running this race, but were at the same time making notes on how to make things better in 1972. To me, that's being organised and I would not pretend to be in that class.

Project Cheers

Captain Shaw was certainly a pivot point: it didn't take an outsider long to appreciate the fact that here was organisation personified. Not to be forgotten, though, is Mrs. Shaw who was always on the spot and kept us well informed by her personal attention to details and hand delivery of last minute messages.

Then one cannot minimize the very important function performed by the Chairman of the Race Committee, Lt Col Odling-Smee. There was one entrant, namely *Cheers*, whose acceptance in the race rested solely on the shoulders of this man. I am confident that had some misfortune befallen *Cheers* the blame, in the public eye, would have descended like a ton of bricks upon LT Col Odling-Smee. In the future perhaps the organisers will consider appointing to the committee a number of international, respected and knowledgeable yachtsmen so as to eliminate the danger of the one-man final decision. Such a committee would have absolute authority to reject any yacht without explanation. In my opinion it has to be a committee where every man has a vote, but where the majority rules and outside pressures, be they political or economic, will not sway the final decision. Anyway, we of project *Cheers* will never forget Jack Odling-Smee and the personal responsibility which he assumed on our behalf.

Throughout the entire period that we spent at Plymouth there appeared to be a continual stream of television people as well as reporters from various newspapers knocking on our door for interviews. Of course as the time got closer to the start, the tempo picked up tremendously. In the earlier stages such interviews fell primarily on Dick's and my shoulders since Tom and Pris were continuing their policy of taking trips out into the country to visit friends.

I am sure that the Follett's escape from Plymouth was not only generated by a sincere desire to see people of past acquaintance, but a strategy on Tom's part to stay away from the milling crowd and the many questions. Admittedly when Tom was giving an interview, whether it was on television or to a reporter, he did a superb job and one standing back looking in at an interview got the feeling that he certainly did not abhor the task at hand. If such an interview were not too lengthy or there were not too many standing in line for 'their turn with the skipper', then Tom exhibited great patience. I would say that he was one of the favorites amongst those doing the interviewing.

We had one small problem aboard *Cheers* which concerned appearance more than anything else. The waters in the Millbay Docks, as is so often the case in an area of sea-going commerce, were very still and had the usual oil film on top. This film was building up hourly on the bottom of *Cheers* and was causing us some grief. In addition, there was a lot of coal dust about and it was almost impossible to step aboard *Cheers* without leaving very permanent footprints on her deck. It was just ground in, impossible to wash away, and of course even if the pattern left by the footprints was to your liking, yellow and black did not really blend. It got to the point where I became very insistent that anyone -- and I meant anyone -- who boarded *Cheers* did so in his stocking feet, his shoes being left on the deck on *Andiamo*.

At long last the morning of the 28th May arrived. Question—would the taking-off-the-shoes-requirement apply to the Race Committee? It certainly would! We had no idea how long they would be questioning Tom and surveying *Cheers*. We had noticed on some yachts of the more conventional type that the survey team came aboard and in a matter of a few minutes had accomplished their mission and were on to the next boat. Their procedure on the more unconventional types took a much longer time.

It was a very cool, bright sunny day and right at the appointed hour, the Race Committee, led by Lt Col Odling-Smee, were invited aboard *Andiamo* and in turn, welcomed aboard *Cheers*. I guess because of previous visits, Jack Odling-Smee fell immediately in the routine of taking off his shoes. The other members were most hesitant and as I turned to one member of the Race Committee who was immediately behind Jack and asked if he would remove his shoes, he in turn said to Odling-Smee: 'Is he serious?' The reply was: 'Of course he is; you won't catch cold.' Every member of the project team was on *Andiamo*'s deck and I was not surprised to see that she was showing a 15° list to starboard! The other members swallowed hard at the 'shoe incident': 'Who does this Morris think he is? We've all worked so hard getting over here and now he's going to blow it because he doesn't want a little more coal dust ground into the decks of *Cheers*. In any case everything worked out satisfactorily and to the best of my knowledge, there were no verbal complaints. The members of the Committee asked Tom several questions and looked over the construction of *Cheers*. There appeared to be no great discussion or

Project Cheers

delving into any one question asked, and literally 15 minutes later, the Race Committee re-traced their footsteps, laced up their shoes, and were on their way—still no inkling as to our acceptance.

Jack Odling-Smee merely smiled and one member, a boat-builder of note and very highly respected by all yachtsmen, Mr. Mashford, turned to Dick Newick and congratulated him not only on *Cheers* design but her very obviously superb construction and quality of workmanship. No suggestions were made as to alterations and so at that very moment, what had been a dream and caused one member I know to loose 15 lbs over the previous year came to fruition. Question--how could we any longer feel in doubt that we, with many others, would officially start?

We had been accepted.

So we poured drinks and a rousing '*Cheers!*' could be heard from the far corner of the Millbay docks.

Actually by the morning of our acceptance the project team for *Cheers* was completely ready to go. We all had our itineraries well planned out. Amazingly enough, everything seemed to be on schedule.

Almost hourly Tom and *Cheers* were receiving many generous gifts of food and beverage from friends as well as commercial interests, all of which were gratefully received. But we just didn't know where we would put it all as *Cheers* waterline was already submerged.

There were always the heartwarming remarks by the interested public who would come down in the late afternoon or early evening so as to look over the entire racing fleet. Some would walk by *Cheers* and shake their heads in dismay; others wanted so anxiously to have a few words with someone who they thought represented that very strange and admitted unconventional object moored off the starboard side of *Andiamo*. Whether the general public thought we were fool-hardy, nuts, or sincerely dedicated in our undertaking, they all wished us well. In a way I guess we became very presumptuous in feeling that we had quite a following of well wishers and prayerful people on our behalf.

Even the wagering populace of England seemed to find *Cheers* of great interest for Ladbrokes, one of the renowned English bookmakers, had taken upon itself to accept wagers on the Race. On our arrival in England -- way back when -- the odds for *Cheers* to win were 25 to 1. They were nothing to brag about, but if you had your money where your sentiments were, the odds could be very rewarding. Even our group could not refrain from putting a few pounds on *Cheers'* possible success. I'll never forget after hearing that Ladbrokes was making odds on the Race that I ventured into a bookmakers just to find out what the odds were at that moment on *Cheers*. All of this betting on a national basis is very new to me and upon entering the bookmakers, I asked the lady behind the cage what the odds were on *Cheers*. After quite a while as she thumbed through many reams of papers, she very courteously replied: 'That dog or horse is not running today.' A perfect squelch. It wasn't until we arrived in Newport that I saw a published report that *Cheers* odds to win had dropped from 25 to 1 to 6 to 1.

The oil slick was building up on *Cheers* so each evening prior to the Race we had hired skin-divers to scrub her down. Their enthusiasm was unquestioned and their labours were very evident but the oil slick was getting the better of us.

On the evening before the Race the Lord Mayor of Plymouth and his wife had invited the participants and those closely associated with the Race to a grand reception.

It was a fun party. By this time we had received so many wires of good wishes and congratulations that if they alone could have won the Race for *Cheers*, she already would have been in first place.

Not only were there letters and telegrams, but magnums of champagne, one of which the Arid Yacht Club of Denver, Colorado, had arranged to have delivered and which was popped by the team with gracious toasts at an informal dinner party after the Lord Mayor's reception.

While attending the Lord Mayor's party, I noted I had not seen Tom for quite a while. I had a couple of telegrams of good wishes directed to his attention that I wanted to deliver, but I couldn't find him. I had no doubt I would see him the next morning, but these messages conveyed nice thoughts which I felt Tom should have before the evening had expired. A gavel sounded and silence came over the ballroom as the Lord Mayor was introduced and he welcomed us all. He wished the contestants 'fair winds'. As is customary, there was to be a response by one of the contestants on behalf of all. To my amazement, Follett gave the response -- I knew then where he was located -- at the head table.

How exciting it would be if I were able to relate that the morning of 1st June 1968 was something spectacular. In truth it was not. Oh, we may have got up a few hours earlier and, granted, we were going to the start of the race, but things had been so arranged as far as *Cheers* was concerned, that the 'immediate family' of *Cheers* would meet for breakfast, would check out of the hotel and return to *Andiamo* so as to be ready to leave the Millbay Docks on or about 8.30 a.m. A multitude of guests had been invited to participate in the start by coming aboard *Andiamo* so as to have a vantage point near the starting line at 11. 00. There were no late comers. Each entrant who wished to be towed to the assembly area behind the starting line had a tow available. Since we were fortunate enough to have a small dinghy that could tow *Cheers* adequately, we elected to go over by our own power. What started out, weather-wise, to be a questionable morning was not in doubt for too long for a continual mist -- in US terms a downpour -- began, continued, and only periodically allowed us a few minutes of uninterrupted drizzle, mist and fog. Literally hundreds of people were standing along the entrance to Millbay Docks and as each boat was towed out to sea, irrespective of their size, nationality or probable placing in the Race, seemed to recognise that they were looking at a champion and could not help but speed him on. Dick Newick, Hank Chamberlain, and I, along with our mutual good friends, Monty Montgomery, editor of Multi-Hull International and Rod MacAlpine-Downie, towed *Cheers* to the assembly area. Pris Follett had gone aboard Ian Major's launch; Pat Newick and Tootie Morris were aboard *Andiamo* with her twenty-six acquired guests.

I was utterly amazed at the number of people on the shoreline, the breakwaters, and in private craft all around us. It was fantastic -- not just hundreds but thousands. Wherever you looked, there was either someone standing on shore, a spectator boat trying to maneuver to a better advantage, and many aircraft circling. Why there were no accidents I'll never understand.

There literally was no wind and all our preparations prior to the Race in case there should be a blow and a fast start were for naught. We had arranged with our friend, Fidler Jennings, of the Royal-Marines, that should the start become congested and confused because of spectator boats, he would personally see that *Cheers* would be defended against the onslaught and would not be interfered with. You must remember that *Cheers* is not a maneuverable craft in close quarters and once she gets up a head of steam, one had best think twice before getting in her way. Fidler was cognizant of this potential and, as *Cheers* crossed the starting line, with little or no wind, a contingent of Royal Marines still saw fit to keep the public away.

Tom crossed the starting line 11 minutes after 'the Gun' and perhaps somewhere in twelfth position. Several hours later as we were still following alongside in our dinghy, he had worked himself into perhaps 3rd or 4th place. By this time Dick and I had been able to get Pat and Tootie off *Andiamo* so as to follow Tom as he passed the breakwaters and headed out to sea. We were quite envious of Tom, on his own and munching one of his sandwiches. He now says he would have shared his sandwiches with us but was afraid to have anything handed between our two boats. Throughout all this time Tom was conversing with many spectators who passed by in their motor launches, acknowledging their good wishes.

Tom was comfortable and we in the launch were miserable. It was time for us to be on our way to Newport. Just before we said farewell to Tom and as he passed one of many large spectators yachts, we heard over the yacht's loudspeaker: 'Good luck Tom. You certainly deserve to win.' What a perfect way for *Cheers* to leave Plymouth and for us, the support team to leave this most generous community of Plymouth and its enthusiastic yachting public.

Our dinghy turned around and headed back towards The Royal Western to say farewell to our many friends, and by 4:00 p.m. on 1st June, the Newicks and Morris's were on their way so as to return to London and eventually, Newport. Four days later the Newick-Morris portion of the team was flying westward over the Atlantic, Pris to follow in a week or so as would the Majors.

Project Cheers

5. Dick Newick makes some last minute adjustments to one of the masts prior to the launching. *Photo Fritz Henle*

Project Cheers

6. The launch. *Photo Fritz Henle*

Chapter seven

A beautiful third place

The recuperation period, which we all enjoyed, certainly had its telling effects upon our countenance. Once again there was an air of anticipation and excitement. Ocean Vista at Newport was to be our new home for the many days that lay ahead, we hoped no longer than about 25th June. As things worked out, the last members of the project team left Newport on 8th July, slightly off schedule but passable under the circumstances.

The only thing that we knew about Ocean Vista was what we had received as literature and from the brochure, we were confident that the arrangements would be fine. This was an understatement for they were superb. Our new residence was a refurbished as well as rearranged home, reminiscent of the grandeur of Newport in years past, a house which had some thirty-five separate rooms designed in a Swiss chalet air with several acres of well dressed lawn, shrubs and trees. It was located a comfortable walking distance from the Ida Lewis Yacht Club and depending upon which room one occupied, with a view of the harbor.

The Ida Lewis Yacht Club was the official representative of the Royal Western Yacht Club of England for the contestants. Bill Thomas who had previously, with his wife been in England at the start of the Race, was on hand at the Ida Lewis to welcome us, together with the Club's hospitable Commodore G. Bogart Blakeley. Needless to say, there was little that the Ida Lewis could do for those who had arrived on the scene awaiting their boat except, as best they could, keep us posted on the latest information concerning 'sighted' yachts. At best no Transtlantic crosser was expected before the 21st or 22nd June and so our arrival at Newport was somewhat premature.

If you took a consensus of opinion today from the Project 68 as to where we spent more time perhaps standing around gazing out to sea, kibitzing with others mutually concerned in the whereabouts of their yachts, it would have to be one location -- the Port-O'-Call, the marina where the contestants would officially check in, clear through Customs, and for the first time in several weeks converse face to face with another human being.

The entire marina was operated by an enthusiastic yachtsman; Pete Dunning. He and his associates were performing as they had at the end of the '64 Race.

At the Port-O'-Call, in addition to many slips for yachts, he had available very attractive rooms some of which upon our arrival were already occupied by members of the press, John Groser, the very capable representative of *The Observer*, and a wife or two of various contestants in the Race. Pete was in constant radio contact with the Coast Guard and you could just tell by his demeanor that everything was well in hand.

If anyone was going to hear about any boat first, Pete would be the man. It was evident that he had a great rapport with the United States Coast Guard and I shall never forget that it was Pete who called us at Ocean Vista at 11:15 on the morning of 27th June and in a very methodical as well as controlled voice relayed to us the first official sighting of *Cheers* 25 yards off the Nantucket lightship.

Don't ask me whether I would rather wait to hear from Tom on his arrival in England, for our final acceptance in the Race, or for Tom to arrive in Newport; I honestly have no preference and I'm confident others of the *Cheers* team would agree. In no case is the waiting game an enjoyable game and in no way do I need to dramatise this aspect of Project 68. The cold, hard facts of the case are that waiting is a most difficult task, literally sapping you of all your energies.

By Sunday 23rd we were almost at our breaking point. There was certainly nothing encouraging in the way of news about any of the boats, except that *Sir Thomas Lipton* had arrived and had been proclaimed the winner.

Selfishly this was no great moment of rejoicing for the project team; we still did not know of *Cheers* whereabouts. However the entire air, whether one was young or old, was improved the very moment when Pete Dunning called and said that *Cheers* had been sighted. No longer was it a dreary day and no longer was it routine. Dick immediately got out his pencil and figured that under reasonable conditions, *Cheers* would arrive Newport about midnight of the 27th. I commandeered a couple of boats so as to go out in the early evening of that day and make sure that we gave Tom a proper welcome. At this particular moment, *Voortrekker* had not been heard from for several days; her whereabouts were most uncertain, and a rather exuberant anticipation developed not only amongst our team but among so many at the Port-O'-Call because *Cheers* was possibly in second place. If all went well, we certainly would know before day's end.

I took it upon myself to call Jack Odling-Smee who was then the house guest of Mr. and Mrs. Thomas. I was not boasting but rather for my own peace of mind, was trying to keep him posted of the current happenings. He was so very enthusiastic and almost apologetically asked if there would be room aboard one of our boats to go out and meet Tom. We would have made room even if we had had to leave the youngsters at home.

The weather at Newport for most of the 27th was nothing to brag about though it did not disturb us as it had in the past. As the hour of departure to go out to look for Tom came closer, the elements got worse. At 8.00 p.m. on the evening of 27th June, two boats loaded with enthusiastic and expectant supporters of *Cheers* left the Port-O'-Call and headed for the finish line at Brenton Tower. Foul weather gear was the order of the day. We divided the group up, Dick leading the pack and I in the other boat following; communications between the two boats was by walkie-talkie. The fog and the rain were certainly in evidence and visibility was 100 yards at best.

As the two motor launches approached the finish line, and the fog lifted a little out of nowhere came *Voortrekker*. I am sure that we all spotted her simultaneously and maybe for a very brief moment which Bruce Dalling I am sure would not deny us, there was disappointment. There was also excitement, for the project team of *Cheers* was on the line to meet and to welcome to Newport a great competitor and a newfound friend. Upon seeing our flotilla, Bruce dropped his sails and Dick Newick's motor launch went alongside to give him the splendid news of his second place. I have never seen an athlete and sportsman so absolutely exhilarated. Dick's launch then returned to the finish line to wait for *Cheers*. By now it was 10.00 p.m., with the fog creeping in, the rain coming down and the seas working up to quite a pitch. Still no *Cheers* and yet we knew she was not too far away. About midnight on both boats we had quite a few people

Project Cheers

who, rightly so, were ready to retire. Our fuel supply was low so we returned to Port-O'-Call.

Some went directly to Ocean Vista to retire and await a new day, others were game and, after refueling, went back to the finish line in one boat. It was perhaps 2 a.m. on the 28th and visibility was no more than 50 ft. The sea was really making up and the weather was absolutely miserable. Still no *Cheers*. We returned to Port-O'-Call and called it quits for the night. No one said a word, but disappointment was written on every face.

Priscilla, particularly, was utterly exhausted. We retired to Ocean Vista, exchanged a few words of pleasantry and encouragement, and we climbed the stairs to our rooms, wondering only when we would see *Cheers*.

It seemed only a few minutes, though it was really a couple of hours, when the public phone rang in Ocean Vista and Mrs. Simms was awakened. Over the loudspeaker in my room, I heard: 'Mr. Morris, the Coast Guard is calling.' I'm not sure in what attire I stumbled down the stairs but who cares? Bill Muessel in charge of the Coast Guard told me that a pilot boat had spotted *Cheers* and asked if Dick Newick and I would like to come out to the station so as to go aboard a Coast Guard launch to take her in tow.

Tom had finished; it was 28th June.

To this day Tom reports his elapsed time as being 27 days, 20 minutes. Officialdom contends that it is 27 days, 13 minutes. We of Project *Cheers* could care less. Tom had arrived in third place, joining the distinguished ranks of those who had beaten the previous Single Handed Transatlantlc record, and was also the first American yacht ever to finish. My, oh my, how proud we were. Tootie drove Dick and me to the Coast Guard station so as to assist them in towing *Cheers* to the Port-O'-Call. At the same time the 'troops' were awakened and were assembled so as to greet Tom at dockside. It was no more than a half-hour after leaving the Coast Guard station when we first saw Tom on radar and then through the mist. It was as though *Cheers* were saying: 'I've been waiting for you. Where have you been?' We had either been at the wrong place at the right time or we were just late!

It was quite amazing, yet in a way not totally unexpected, to see Tom looking his very natural self and with absolutely no appearance of strain, stress or excessive tiredness!

The Coast Guard launch came alongside *Cheers*. Dick and I reached over the rail, to shake Tom's hand, and congratulate him on his success. Admittedly it was third place, but what a beautiful third place it was.

Can you imagine all those disappointed people throughout the 'wagering world' who had bet *Cheers* might not even finish? Perhaps Tom showed some degree of disappointment on learning of his third place but here again it was evident that we were in the company of a champion for though he knew of *Sir Thomas Lipton*'s success, he had not really heard of Bruce Dalling's arrival. Immediately we told him of *Voortrekker's* coming in a few hours previous, he simply said: 'Jolly good. It's evident that Bruce sailed an excellent Race.' Perhaps within a half-hour or so *Cheers* was under tow and just off the pier of Port-O'-Call. As the Coast Guard launch gently nudged *Cheers* alongside the dock Pris Follett was an absolute image of a sunburst. It has been quoted elsewhere that the policeman on watch at the Port-O'-Call commented: 'Gee, he must be nuts to have sailed that thing'. We certainly didn't think so.

Previous to Tom's arrival we of Project *Cheers* had had the pleasure and good fortune of having Heywood Hale Broun and Bud Lamoreaux, both of CBS pay us a visit and spend quite a bit of time, participating anxiously with the rest in the waiting game. Both of these gentlemen, good friends of Priscilla and Tom, were most enthusiastic and eager in wanting to feature Tom in the next day's program, CBS Saturday News. Pris had had the forethought to alert CBS so they were at dockside as *Cheers* peeked through the early morning fog. Thus the arrival of *Cheers* in Newport is well documented by the professionals. By then it must have been 7.00 a.m. on 28th June. Tom was but a few minutes' drive from a warm shower, good food, and a well deserved rest; however it was necessary to comply with the formality of clearing Customs and because of this, a slight delay occurred. Even before the Customs Officer arrived, all documentation had been completed in true Follett fashion, and thus it was a mere formality with an exchange of papers, a few words of congratulations, and a sincere 'welcome home' on behalf of the United States Government. From the Port-O'-Call, the entourage moved to Ocean Vista, the hero, the followers, the film historians.

Project Cheers

By then Ocean Vista was the headquarters for *Cheers* and even at that very early hour, it seemed to be vibrating with the anticipated arrival of the celebrity. Eloise Simms was so thoughtful and foresighted that the downstairs of their home was made available for our use. Coffee and a light breakfast was available to those who possibly could think at that moment of their earthly needs. The champagne which Dick had purchased days before was finally consumed in the same manner as on 12th December 1967, and on the evening of 31st May 1968, a rousing '*Cheers*' was echoing throughout Ocean Vista and all Newport.

Tom was home.

Before the early morning festivities had ended, Tom was strumming on a guitar, so reminiscent of the night before he sailed from St Croix to England, unimpressed by his success, unassuming in his demeanor and pleased to be home and once again entertaining his friends. Where the remainder of the day went I would not know.

Tom was eager to complete the circle and wanted very much to sail *Cheers* to Christiansted so on the 8th July 1968, Tom left Newport. By now the Newicks were on their way home; Pris was about to leave for California; the Morrises were to return to Denver. I don't know how often one has to say farewell to Tom Follett and *Cheers* to not acquire a lump in his throat and a prayer to the Almighty that they will have a safe journey. I would imagine, though, that we who are categorised as sentimentalists will never experience anything different. Clearly *Cheers* was a proven ocean racer and a 'nip' down to the Virgin Islands, a matter of some 1,200 miles, would appear to many as but a weekend junket. Certainly being around Tom Follett and Dick Newick, you might get hardened to this type of casualness, but they haven't yet indoctrinated me as a full-fledged member.

Somewhere along the way I'm sure I have wondered what that last moment would be like when *Cheers* was heading homeward, the project team having fulfilled its mission; Tootie and I would be alone, reflecting on the immediate past. I suspect if I were an accomplished writer or a man eloquent with words that I could share with you these very personal thoughts but I do not qualify and thus ask that you bear with me and in essence write the last sentence. Perhaps just recalling a fond farewell or a moment of thankfulness will in itself paint you a word picture of our feelings and emotions. As someone has said: 'This, too, will pass', and so the closing chapter of Project 68 is written.

Not too long ago Dick Newick presented me with a beautiful color photo of *Cheers*. Tootie and I have admired it but it was only the other day when we took it to have it framed that I observed an inscription on the back: '*Cheers* To Tootie and Jim who made it all possible. Dick.'

The Morrises in turn have always felt: *Cheers* to Dick and Tom who allowed us to share in their dream and their success.

Postscript

A thought or two....

I am quite confident that what the project team has experienced will, for us, not be repeated. This is certainly of no great consequence in itself. We have been involved in an event which we hope will be continued. It is with this in mind that I encroach on the future and record a thought or two.

I would not like my remarks to be interpreted to give the impression that I am absolutely against the element of commercial sponsorship. I am sure that this type of backing, as long as it is in good taste and handled with discretion has its place in the world of yachting, though just where and under what conditions I have yet to come to a conclusion. I am at this time led somewhat to believe that its place is unto itself-a separate race where the highly sponsored, the 'big boys' of the yachting world with few or no restrictions can compete in the crossing of the Atlantic on an equal basis; that is if the availability of money is the first criterion.

However, if you are one who believes strongly and fervently in the original concept of the Single-Handed Transatlantic Race, and I am now speaking of the spirit in which it was conceived, you must find it very difficult to accept compromise and say that within the same race sponsored and unsponsored should be pitted against each other. I agree that, as evidenced by this past race, the 'development of suitable boats, gear, supplies and techniques for single-handed crossing under sail' will most likely develop more quickly because of sponsorship.

It does take a lot of money to develop, campaign and race an oceangoing yacht so as to cross the Atlantic in good time. However, I am more concerned with what I think is the true objective of the race in its fullest concept; that it is a 'sporting event'. This is paramount in my mind. If only by chance it encourages the other purposes more quickly this is fine. I have no crystal ball, but I cannot help but envisage that by 1972 the individual, the small boat and the under-financed will be has-beens. Only if they are dreamers will they think seriously of being participants-that is participants who realistically think they have a chance of winning. I offer some answers to questions, which I am already confident the sponsor and organisers are thinking about and will be confronted with in the future. Admittedly this is at its best a rather negative approach on my part. I am hopeful, however, that to whatever extent sponsorship is allowed and to whatever extent world-wide criticism must be endured by the Race Committee they will never lose sight of the fact that this race and perhaps this race alone does afford the imaginative designer, the spirited and competent skipper, a would-be sponsor, at least the opportunity of giving it a try.

Admittedly the risk and all that implies is always there. For me, however, the intriguing aspect of this race and the races of the future, will be that the rules and regulations are few in number, but put a premium on seaworthiness and seamanship.

Part two

The story according to T. Follett

Project Cheers

The story according to Tom Follett

Chapter one

Early trials

The thought of a transatlantic race (or any other race) as crew leaves me cold and not only because of the temperatures often encountered, i.e. it just doesn't *send* me. But the old blood starts to run warm when you begin to talk about 'Single-Handed Transatlantic Races' and the question of entering pops up. Why? I haven't the slightest idea.

I'm no racing type: no single-handed type either. I hate sailing in the high latitudes where the temperature is low, the atmosphere foggy and the winds are fluky. Now and then I'll willingly go as far north as Bermuda if the weather is fine but I like the sun and constant winds and would just as soon do nothing but cruise in the West Indies between Grenada and the Virgin Islands with an occasional round the island race to provide a good excuse for a beach party. Oh well, I got into the 1968 Single-Handed Transatlantic Race in spite of all my inclinations to keep warm and, oddly enough, I enjoyed the experience. I had a good boat.

I began to seriously consider the possibility of entering the race about 2 ½ years ago when I planned to build a trimaran to one of Dick Newick's designs. I had sailed some long passages on the prototype Trice and I liked her and thought she might do well against competition. I didn't then think I'd be able to make it in the 1968 race since I had no boat building experience and thought it would take me a good three years to come up with something worth while. But I did feel relatively sure about getting into the 1972 race.

I met Axel Pederson in New York about that time and found out from him how to go about entering and got some good dope on courses to avoid. Seems it took Axel a long time to finish the 1964 race in his yacht *Marco Polo* because of lack of wind.

OK. I had the idea to enter. Why keep quiet about it? No secret really. So -- Dick Newick knew I was considering the possibility and,

Project Cheers

maybe, this got him started thinking about the design of a winning boat.

In the spring of 1967 some sketches arrived from Dick with a request for comments. These sketches were the basis of his idea for a boat to win the race and the design was proposed to a South African friend of his with the thought that she would be built in South Africa as a South African entry for the 1968 race.

I didn't see how the boat could be built and the bugs ironed out in time to enter in 1968 but I did like what I saw on the sketches. So I wrote to Dick that, if his South African buddy wasn't interested or had other fish to fry, I liked the looks of the boat and would be available to sail her if we could get her ready in time. I was then living in Coconut Grove, Florida and there was usually a delay of about a week, while letters went to and fro between St Croix and the Grove, before we could sort out any given question. Also, being in the yacht delivery business, I am frequently away from home for long periods and this is no help to communication. We managed, under this handicap, very well I thought. It turned out the man in South Africa had other things on his mind and I was elected to be the crew provided we could get the boat built.

I think it must have been early in April of 1967 when Dick and I decided to go ahead. But it wasn't as simple as all that. First, we needed money and neither of us had it in sufficient quantity. Fortunately, along came a friend from Denver, Colorado -- Jim Morris, who lives in St Croix part of the time -- with some extra dollars in his pocket and the good sense to spend it on something worthwhile. We both accepted his offer of assistance -- were, indeed, overjoyed to get it -- and the three of us became a group which we called 'Project 68'. Dick Newick to design and build the boat. Jim Morris to oversee the operation and to make sure it all ran along in a businesslike manner and myself to do the trials and to sail the boat in the 1968 Single-Handed Transatlantic Race from Plymouth, England to Newport, Rhode Island, USA. Both Jim and I to do all we could to help Dick get the necessary materials to St Croix for the building job.

My wife thought I was a bit of a nut to enter the race in an experimental boat and dragged her feet somewhat at first. But she gradually became resigned to the idea and, later on, maybe even enthusiastic especially after she saw the boat for the first time in England. Even for someone who knows nothing about boats, *Cheers* catches the eye and the imagination. Priscilla and I lived on a yacht of our own for about five years, part of the time in the Mediterranean and part of the time in the West Indies, so boats are no novelty to her.

In July, 1967 I sent in my entry application to the race committee along with a cheque for the fee. Some of the early sketches went along plus a short discussion of the boat and its rig as we then saw it. The Race Committee showed no particular enthusiasm and they returned my entrance fee with the word they didn't think our entry could be accepted. The three of us felt differently, however, and decided to go ahead with the project and try to convince the committee, as we went along, that our boat could qualify.

Two big questions at the time were seaworthiness and accommodation (or the lack thereof). Seaworthiness did present us with a problem, adequately solved, but accommodation was no trouble. For me it was enough. A tomb approximately 2 ½ ft wide by 14 ft long with a seat in the centre, a fabric berth in one end and a table in the other. Standing headroom in the middle under a plexiglass and fabric hatch. More than enough space for me to take along everything I wanted except a piano.

In October, Dick reckoned he could launch the boat, ready for her first sea trials, early in December. Originally, the plan was to get it in the water in November but this was impractical owing to the difficulty of getting materials to St Croix. Launch date finally turned out to be 12th December 1967 which, I considered, was a most speedy job. Not only a fast job but a job well done with the boat looking good and the construction first class.

My wife and I used to live in England. Only way to keep warm over there is to spend a lot of time in the pubs. People are saying '*Cheers*' every now and then and it's all very nice. I rather liked the expression and got to signing my letters with '*Cheers*' rather than 'yours truly' or 'yours faithfully' or 'sincerely yours' or drivel like that. Morris and Newick apparently liked the expression too and thought -- 'why not call the new boat *Cheers*?' -- So we did.

December came along and I was in St Croix after completing the delivery of a trimaran from Ft Lauderdale, Florida to St Thomas. *Cheers*

Project Cheers

was a beauty. Painted yellow with a red bottom -- two red bottoms -- and looking very fast sitting outside the building shed.

Launch day. 12th December 1967. Plenty of people standing around ready to help and, in most cases, actually helping. Oddly enough -- not the usual shouting out of unwanted advice on how best to do the job. Photographers grinding away with their cameras. Ian Major and Dave Dana over from St Thomas for the day. Dick Eames and Henry Chamberlain standing by to lend a hand. Wally Galloway and Bernard Rhodes appeared to be satisfied with the job they had done and they had good cause to be so. Pat Newick was there and Tootie Morris was ready to break a bottle of champagne.

Not far from the building shed to the water. Popped the boat -- sans masts -- onto a borrowed trailer and wheeled it down to the beach. More people came over to watch. Step the masts. One doesn't fit. Oy, vey! Newick whips a plane out of his pocket and starts shaving off wood. Easy there amigo -- not too much. OK -- it fits. Bend on the sails. Tootie Morris (Jim's wife) breaks a bottle of champagne over one bow (stern??) and rushes off to the local hospital. That bottle glass is sharp, sister. Have to look out for flying bits. We stand around and drink champagne while the Morris leg is being stitched up. Tootie returns to the scene still smiling and downs a pint of champagne to kill the pain and to catch up with the rest of us. Falls down dead drunk. We kick her to one side and push the boat in the water. Not much surf. Stick in the dagger boards. Powerboat ready to tow us out beyond the reef. Off we go!

The boat floats. Not only does it float but it sails. A bit difficult since some of the things are sort of haywired together but good enough for us to tell we have something worth while on our hands. Dick Newick, Jim Morris and I aboard for the first go. We get a tow far out beyond the reef to give us plenty of time to maneuver and the sails go up. Bit of a problem there. Slot in the lee side of the mast to take the luff rope not a practical thing. Much too difficult to get the sail up and then there's the problem of taking it off again. Must take the thing out of the slot when lowering and there's the whole business to do over again when it's time to hoist once more. Can't have that.

Dagger boards a hell of a job. Partly because they aren't complete and partly because they're held in place with wedges and partly because there's no place to stand when pulling them in and out of the case and partly because we really don't know what we're doing anyway. First thing to see to is another arrangement for the luff of the sails. Second thing is the dagger boards. Third is steering. A rod to the tillers and to a stick amidships appears to be unsatisfactory.

No non-skid paint anywhere on the boat. Like an ice skating rink. Jim Morris falls in the water. Is rescued. And so endeth the first lesson. We sail into Christiansted Harbor and go alongside Protestant Cay where drinks and food await and there we cool our heels a while and discuss what's to be done. Roller reefing is a dead loss. A gooseneck which will permit the booms to rotate about the masts more than 180 degrees as well as wind up the sail looks feasable on paper. On a boat -- on *Cheers*, that is -- it looks hopeless and it is hopeless. What to do about that?

Plenty of ideas. Some of them good. Can't do anything much today. Let's go for a sail. So we do. This time -- Jim Morris, Dave Dana and myself. Lines get caught in the dagger boards. Dave falls overboard. We fish him out of the drink. Lots of fun but a damned hard job trying to sail the boat as she is. Takes the three of us nearly the whole ocean to bring *Cheers* about on another tack. Doesn't do to fiddle about in a crowded anchorage under those conditions. Finally -- in we come and the launch day is over. Generally, a success although plenty of modifications to be done before we have a single-handed boat to play with.

When I look back now and think about how much modification we had to do and how long it took us to figure out what was required as well as to get it done, I wonder how anyone can hope to launch a new boat and enter a race a few days later. A stock boat with most of the bugs out -- maybe. A new model -- not for me friend. Give me plenty of time to shake her down.

After the launching I stayed in St Croix until the 19th of December taking the boat out for a few times and discussing with Dick and Jim what needed to be done and waiting around while various changes were being made.

We were doing the initial trials with cheap sails made up out of canvas until we could come to some sort of agreement about what sort of rig was needed or, rather, what sort we could use. Manfred Dietrich, in St Thomas, was doing all our sail work and, as soon as he knew what we wanted, sails were forthcoming in short order. We experienced no delays to amount to anything because of sails and I liked the idea of having a local man available for consultation who was willing to start immediately on the job and keep after it until it was done.

It took us only a little while to conclude that the sails we had were insufficient in area to permit us to work to windward with any speed. Accordingly the foresail and mizzen were increased in area and some jibs were added. The booms had to be lengthened to take the extra length along the foot of the sails and we ended up shortening the luffs a bit to keep the booms clear of the hatch. Jibs had to be set flying and this caused us to have to limit the size a bit more than we should otherwise have done. Setting the things was enough of a problem but, occasionally when the wind piped up, getting them off again was nearly too much for one man.

I mentioned 'foresail' and 'mizzen' above. I like these terms for the two boomed sails as well as any. Which is which depends on which end of the boat is forward at the moment.

By the 19th December we had decided on some modifications and I went off to Coconut Grove for Christmas. Winches were added. One for each boomed sail, one for a jib tack outhaul and one for a jib sheet. A lot of extra weight but definitely necessary in spite of the relatively small sail area. A sleeve was sewn to the sails and this was tried as was a lacing around the mast. The masts were cut down in thickness saving about 60 lbs total weight and, although we felt they could be cut down more, we stopped there owing to the lack of time available to test them to destruction. Spray rails were added and some fairing to the connecting members included as well as a forward platform on which to stand to work the dagger boards. Some work was done on the dagger boards making them more complete and the steering arrangement was changed.

While in Miami, I ordered some track and slides for the sails just in case we should need it. We did and this is what we finally used after trying a slot in the lee side of the mast for the luff rope, a sleeve sewn on the whole way up the luff and a lacing around the mast. Unfortunately, the stainless steel track I sent down from Miami was not very satisfactory but Dick managed to get some good nickel-silver stuff from

7. *Cheers*! (l to r) Pat Newick, Jim Morris, Tom Follett, Dick Newick, Tootie Morris, Dick Eames. Photo Fritz Henle.

8. The team prepares *Cheers* for an early sail. Photo Fritz Henle.

9. Capsize test carried out before sponson was fitted. In calm water *Cheers* floated with her masts horizontal. Photo Newick.

10. This shot of the same capsize test clearly shows how small her wetted surface is. Photo Newick.

11. Looking a bit pensive; Tom Follett prior to setting off on his first solo excursion. Photo Fritz Henle.
12. Tom Follett leaving St. Croix on his first long solo trial. Note the absence of sponson and anti-dive plates. Photo Newick.

13. *Cheers* moving along at a fair clip during early trials off St. Croix. Photo Fritz Henle.
14. *Cheers* on an early trial, showing foresail with an experimental sprit instead of a boom. Number 2 jib is set. Compare this picture with plate 19 which shows *Cheers* with her sponson fitted. Photo Newick

The story according to Tom Follett

St Thomas through Dave Dana and this worked fine with our slides. The stainless had rather sharp edges which bound against the slides and filing them off helped only a little.

On the 10th January 1968 I came back to St Croix to do more trials and I stayed on until the 12th February when we laid *Cheers* up for a major modification.

Neither the sleeve on the luff of the boomed sails nor the lacing around the mast was satisfactory. Might have been OK if the masts had a more constant section to the top but the taper was too much. The sleeve idea was good aerodynamically but a mess in reality. The lacing was simple and this is what we wanted but, it too, looked messy and it was a hard job to get the sails all the way down.

To lick the problem of a gooseneck and, hopefully, to save some weight we tried a sprit rig. Again -- this looks good in theory but turns out to be too much trouble for a single-hander to fiddle with at sea. We finally wound up with an old fashioned boom jaw arrangement such as is used on the old gaff rigged boats and this worked out very well. Simple enough and easy to repair if broken and essentially trouble free. No roller reefing of course. We had Manfred sew in some grommets on the new Dacron sails and I used a lacing around the boom to reef and found this quite handy. Took maybe a little longer than winding the sail on the boom but the sail always set well and the system was much less complicated than a roller gear.

We tried some lines to the tillers and to the midships stick but this was even worse than the rods we started out with. So -- back to the rods with some changes here and there and they worked very well.

Early on in the design stage Dick and I decided it might be a good idea to wait for some trial runs before worrying too much about a self steering gear. The boat looked like being quite stable in direction and this was the case. Trim the sails, adjust the forward dagger board and lock in a little helm one way or the other and she would hold a good course anywhere from a dead run to hard on the wind. A self steering gear for a boat going in both directions is a complicated thing not to mention the extra weight and windage. This was a good break for us.

Until the 20th January we confined our trials to a short distance outside the harbor at Christiansted. We'd be towed out beyond the reef by a power boat and then get sail up and go on about our business from

Project Cheers

there. This was sometimes a rather exciting operation since *Cheers* was so directionally stable it was nearly impossible to change course unless a good head of speed was on. As a result most of the yacht owners in the harbor would reach for their tranquilisers (shot of rum to wash them down) when they saw us preparing to get under way. Those of us on *Cheers* and on the towing boat usually had our hands full. Once we hit the concrete quay a good bang but *Cheers* was rugged and survived her indignities with only a little bit of epoxy putty necessary to conceal the scars. Don't know about the wear and tear on my nerves. Usually we'd sail into the harbor and run downwind to pick up our mooring. Rounding up was out of the question. A time or two we were going at such a clip (even with some crew dragging feet) that we couldn't hold the mooring and then there would be a Chinese Fire Drill to get us stopped before going right the way through a moored yacht. Our big masts had so much windage with the sails off that we never could slow down below about 3 knots unless it was nearly flat calm.

Once I ran into Dick's big power boat and nearly sank him. He was towing me out (only me aboard at the time) of the harbor and I hoisted sails while still inside and sheeted them in. No wind at the time since we were in the lee of a point of land. Just about to round the point going out of the harbor I nipped forward to cast off the tow line and got hit by a gust. Took off like a shot and Dick's diesel engine didn't have my acceleration. Ran about 4 ft of my lee bow right up his ass and hung on like I'd harpooned a whale. Fortunately, the hole was above the water line or Dick would have been hard pressed to keep afloat. Didn't even scratch the paint on *Cheers* . Dangerous business this towboat racket!

Our main difficulty during the first set of trials was lack of wind. In the Virgin Islands one can depend on a good breeze most of the time from late December on through early Spring but, this year, the wind was often no more than 8 to 10 knots. We needed the usual 20 to 25 knots to really find out how the boat would go but were seldom lucky enough to get it. I did manage, on the first shakedown cruise, to pick up some good breeze further down in the West Indies but, by then, we had taken care of most of the changes to the rig and steering.

Jim Morris and I took off for St Thomas (about 40 miles to the north) on 20th January but had to turn back due to lack of wind after three or four hours. We sailed with the outrigger to windward for a while and this worked well enough except for the difficulty of sheeting a jib. Long as we could keep the outrigger out of the water the reduction in wetted surface was enough for us to maintain a respectable speed. This is not really a recommended procedure single handed owing to the necessity of being constantly alert to keep upright. But it's probably OK in light, settled, weather for short periods.

By this time we had drilled some holes in the dagger boards and were using pins to make adjustments rather than wedges and this was a great improvement. The only snag was a lack of fine control. The boat was very sensitive to adjustments of the forward board and, with the pin arrangement, we had too much movement all at once. More pin holes could have solved this problem but might have weakened the boards too much. We settled by using the rudder to provide the necessary fine control to the course and this proved satisfactory.

On the 21st January we tried again for St Thomas with a 15 to 18 knot breeze. This time Jim Morris and Henry Chamberlain were along as well as myself but the wind was out of the north and we were washed off toward Puerto Rico. Could have beat our way over right enough but that would have put us in after midnight I figured so back we came. Nice sail. Decided to forget St Thomas for the time being and pull the boat out of the water to take care of some modifications we had decided on. Although we had plenty of time; we thought we had better push the panic button then rather than waiting until there was a real need for it.

I had been practicing putting the boat around on another tack singlehanded and was then taking about a minute and ten seconds. By then I'd generally fall down on the net gasping for breath and crying out for beer to regain strength. Ropes all over the place and really a jigsaw puzzle to sort them out. Two sets of endless sheets. One set for each boom. This, in itself, enough to form quite a rat's nest around the cockpit. Jib sheet on top of that although often stowed out of the way on a tacking exercise: jib tack outhaul: halyards: bits of string. We tried coloring one set of sheets with dye to help sort them out but the dye washed off to toute de suite and we ended up with one set of braided line and the other of conventional twisted stuff. Even then, especially on a dark night, tacking was always a chore. I got so I could do the job in about thirty seconds by the time I finished the race but only in daylight.

A word or two about tacking a proa -- No doubt there are several systems in existence. In Newport, a chap told me about the proas they use in the Pacific Islands where he spent some time in the Navy. Seems the poor crew man unships the mast from one end when he comes about and carries it to the other end to be set up. All this in how many minutes? Hours? Surely not for racing around the buoys. Our system, as I mentioned before, took me about 30 seconds after I got thoroughly used to it and provided there was enough light to see what went on. The procedure was to let fly the sheets (any jibs must be doused first) and bear off a little. The boat then drifts broadside to the wind making practically no headway. Raise what was the aft dagger board disconnecting the steering linkage first. Stick a pin in the thing to hold it at a height determined by experience. Run ('stagger' is a better word) to the other end and lower the new aft board and connect the steering linkage. Then sheet in the sails and away in the other direction.

The rub with this system is going to windward in cold weather. Standing in the cockpit ready to duck out of the weather is not practical. The boat picks up speed too fast and, before the sheets can be hardened in, spray is finding its way into the accommodation and down the crew man's neck. Best to leave the cockpit buttoned up tight and do everything from up top hoping the oilskin suit will shed most of the water. Of course, another snag comes when trying to get below while charging off to windward. The cockpit has to be unbuttoned and entry made and then re-buttoned before plowing into a big one. This requires some fine timing. I managed it now and then. Mostly then.

Our primary reason for going to St Thomas was to give Manfred a chance to cut some new sails and to put in a fabric berth and to install a fabric top over the plexiglass hatch. We thought it would be nice to have the boat at his place on Hassel Island (in St Thomas harbor) to make it easier for measurements but, after the second attempt with no luck, we asked Manfred to come over by plane when he could and do the measurements in St Croix.

On the 22nd January we hauled the boat out on the beach and took care of some changes and were back in the water the next day. Manfred came over on the 11:00 plane and we went for a sail so he could see what was needed. Then, back to the harbour where measurements were made and Manfred went off back to St Thomas to start work.

The story according to Tom Follett

The new sails arrived on the 1st February and, by that time, we had everything ready to go for the first shakedown cruise. All the odd jobs we could think of were taken care of and we had capsized the boat off the beach to see how it would go. It went passably well I thought. The masts had enough flotation to prevent a 180 degree capsize (a capsize to windward that is). In fact, with two men on the end of each mast they wouldn't dip below the water. It was a bit difficult to get the boat upright again but it looked like it might be possible at sea. After the masts got up about 30 degrees off the water the thing balanced and it took very little to drop it down right side up. Not a particularly happy situation but I didn't worry too much about it. Took about 15 minutes to pump the water out of the weather hull after getting upright again. A Henderson type double action pump sucked the bilges dry very nicely.

Of course a boat like this doesn't actually sink under any conditions. Nothing in it but wood. When capsized 90 degrees the hull only takes in enough water to about half fill it and there you are or, rather, there I am. I managed to capsize on the shakedown cruise and then I found out that we did, indeed, have a problem on our hands.

There were two reasons for the shakedown cruise I started on the 2nd February. I wanted to find out about the boat under actual seagoing conditions and to get a good idea about speed. But I also wanted to know about how much food and water to take with me to England since weight is a big factor in a boat of this type. By this time we had decided to sail the boat to England rather than ship her. The Race Committee was still refusing our entry application and we felt the best demonstration was a seagoing trip of some dimensions. Anyway, by this time, I personally had enough regard for *Cheers* to be reluctant to trust it to the tender mercies of stevedores and shipping concerns.

I planned the shakedown cruise to take me out as far as Barbados in order to get in a good bit of windward work. I had charts for this trip plus stores for a couple of weeks. On 2nd February Dick Newick's power boat *Providencia* towed me out of the harbor and I was on my way.

Red Stolle's new trimaran (a Newick design built in the Canary Islands) *Barco Mañana* was on the way to St Thomas so I thought I'd go over in company with her. Dick and Jim were aboard along with Red and his wife Suttie and all were armed with cameras. We had a good breeze and I got in some good sailing before leaving them off French Cap Cay. Had no trouble sailing circles around *Barco Mañana* without a jib and his log was indicating 9 knots now and then I found out later. Wind generally about 12 to 15 knots but gusting to 20 with rain squalls.

Not long before I started to write down modification data in my log. Water was pouring into the cabin through the bilge pump hose entrances on the side. I set a small jib to make some time to windward and the halyard block carried away after about half an hour. Nothing to get excited about but something to be taken care of eventually.

The wind was out of the east and, off French Cap, I put *Cheers* on the port tack with a course to take me slightly to the south of the island of Saba. By nightfall it was blowing fairly hard and I doused the mizzen to see how it went. Held a course very well and rode quite comfortably hard on the wind. I was pleased with the windward performance with the new sails although it was a bit of a nuisance to lose the jib halyard block on one end so soon.

Didn't sleep much the first night out. An hour here and an hour there. Looking out for shipping and bailing water kept me awake most of the time. But *Cheers* sailed herself and there was no particular physical strain.

The following morning at daylight Saba was aft of the beam and I started to bear off just a bit through the lee of Nevis with the mizzen set. Still a good breeze and we started to move along at a good clip. Nice and easy except for the water coming into the cockpit but that was easily bailed out every now and then and it kept my feet nice and cool. Delightful sailing through the lee of Nevis and Monserrat and, just after dark, I wound up between Basseterre, Guadaloupe and the Isles de Saintes and there I doused all sail and let her drift.

One nice thing about a multi-hull yacht. Drifting without sail is a pleasure. Not so on the average ballasted hull boat. Take sail off and you roll your brains out. Put sail up in a calm and the bloody things slat about tearing off slides and making enough noise to make one prefer the telephone. Drifted very cheerfully all night between Guadaloupe and Dominica and ended up nearly off Portsmouth, Dominica next morning because of a north east wind.

The lee of Dominica was its usual fluky self and I spent a good part of the day trying to work my way through. Toward the south end

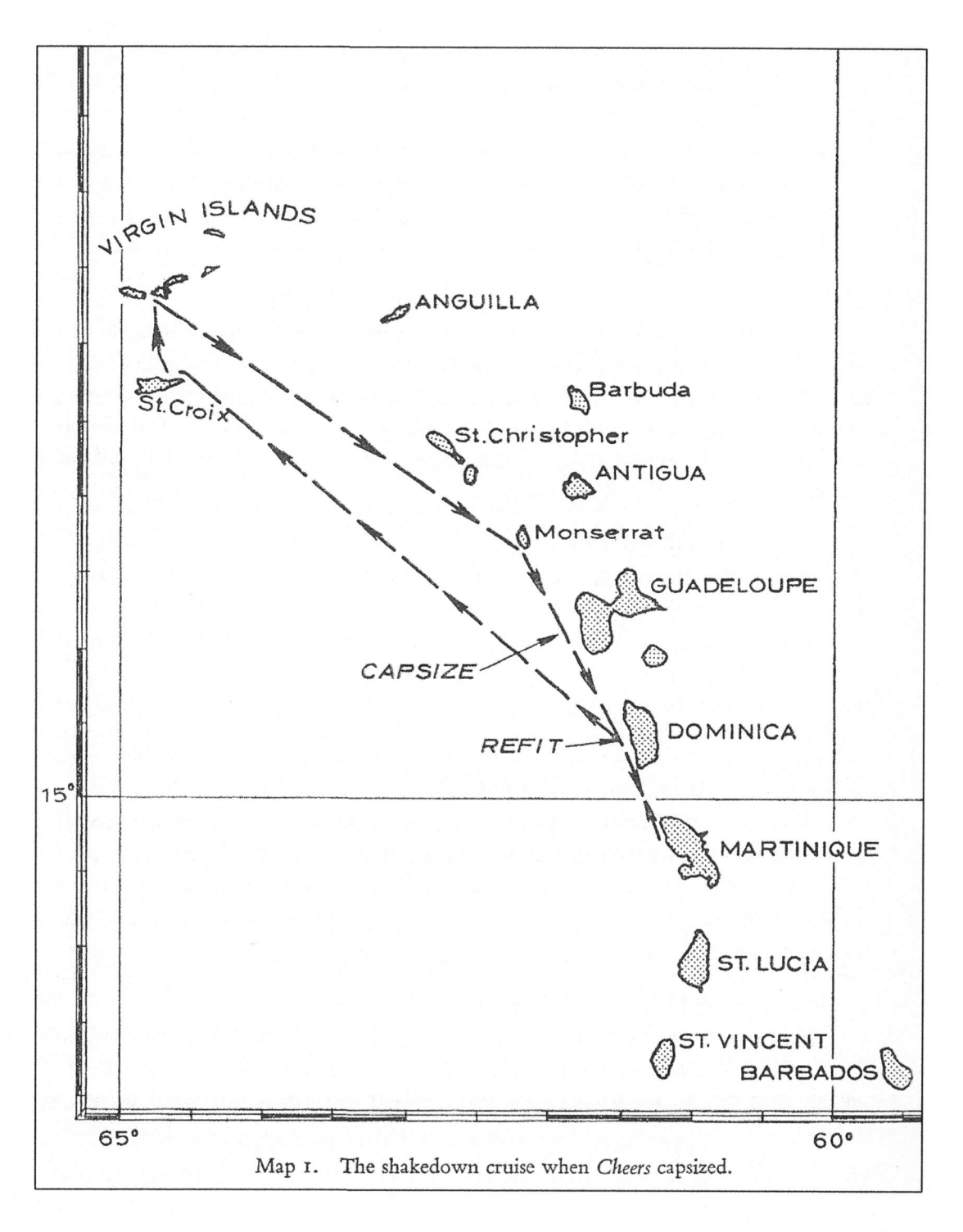

Map 1. The shakedown cruise when *Cheers* capsized.

Project Cheers

(Scott's Head) the wind was often flat calm and a nice popple of sea tossed me here and there in a most annoying manner. The fact that this is the normal thing never seems to decrease the annoyance and I often find myself in a near state of frenzy after working my way through the lee of some West Indian islands in an engineless boat. Dominica always seems to give me the worst time. But the Dominica channel, between Dominica and Martinique, was anything but flat calm. Once around Scott's Head the wind piped up to about 20 knots from the ENE and I reached across to Pt. La Mare in Martinique in 2 ½ hours. A distance of 26 miles. Not such good speed, I thought, but passable.

Thought I'd spend the night in St Pierre Bay so eased in close to shore (deep water here nearly to the beach) and dropped the hook. Sure enough, although practically flat calm, inside an hour the anchor line is straight up and down and I'm drifting out to sea. Let it go. Too much trouble trying to set an anchor. Hauled it in and let the boat drift. More comfortable that way except for having to look out for shipping. Ah, Follett, you shifty character, I detect a sour grapes note here. Is it really more comfortable to drift vs. hanging on a nice snug anchor? Well ... maybe not. But how can you make your anchor snug in St Pierre? Like hanging on to a plate glass window with suction cups on your feet.

Next morning I hoisted sails and headed back for the Dominica channel. Looked like here was the best wind and sea conditions I could hope for and I wanted to make some runs between good check points to see how fast I could go. Also, it was a close reach from Martinique to Dominica and I wanted that run particularly. The sea was rough in the channel and this was also what I wanted.

So -- on 5th February I had a good run across the Dominica channel to Scott's Head. Worked my way through the lee of Dominica again and headed out for Guadaloupe in the early evening. Another nice run from Prince Rupert Bay, Dominica to the Saintes and from there to Guadaloupe with some good check points for speed on both a close and a broad reach. On the way back on the starboard tack, I could use a jib since my halyard block on that end was OK.

Just north of Basseterre, Guadaloupe about 2200 hours. Light breeze from ENE. Foresail and mizzen up. Foresail vanged down with sheets eased a bit. Small jib up. Dozed off. A rattling noise and water around my head. Crawl out of the cockpit to see what's going on and, lo, I'm capsized to 90 degrees.

Here's what probably happened; wind dropped off very light as often happens in the lee of the islands. Boat rounds up and goes through the wind. Gust comes down off the mountains (and sometimes these gusts have a lot of power in them) and hits me on the wrong side and over I go in a hurry.

OK. What to do now? Sails off. Get things stowed as well as possible. Try and get the thing upright again. No dice. Climb up the net to the outrigger. No good. Jump on the dagger board. No good. Wind only moderate and not too much sea running. Lights of Basseterre visible in the distance. Nothing to do but cool my heels and 'cool' is the right word here. Warm tropical night and nice warm water but, in wet clothing, it's no picnic. Makes me shudder to think what the North Atlantic must be like under similar circumstances. Also, with the boat capsized to 90 degrees, there's not much living space. I wedged myself on the side of the deck box but in a not very comfortable position. Best I could do, though, other than crawl into the cabin and sit submerged in the water. Not a bad idea provided it only lasts an hour or so but, for days at a time, not very practical.

Wind picked up a bit and sea began to build as I drifted out toward the southwest. Figured in four or five months I'd probably wind up in Colombia or Venezuela if the wind held out of the northeast but didn't see how my rations could hold out that long. Started to bite my fingernails.

About 0300 the next morning I spotted a ship not too far off shore and flashed him an sos with my waterproof flashlight. No answer and he carried on off into the distance. Started to bite my toenails.

About half an hour before sunrise another ship comes along and he sees my sos and things begin to look a bit brighter. It's a good thing these waterproof lights are indeed waterproof or I should likely still be in the Caribbean drifting around with no one to play chess with. Well - maybe a fisherman would have spotted me anyhow but I was really glad to see the *M/V Novelist* (T. & J. Harrison Line) out of Liverpool under the command of Capt W. G. Jackson.

Fortunately the third officer, on watch at the time, had sharp eyes and knew what an sos was and woke the skipper. Very often being rescued at sea is worse than the ailment itself. I must say that, when I saw the lightly loaded *Novelist* sticking a mile high out of the water and bearing down on me, I mentally wrote off *Cheers* as kindling wood for the fires of Guadaloupe. Not so. The ship comes to a stop very nicely just a few feet away. A line is passed and made fast to the outrigger and led to a forward winch in an attempt to pull me upright. No can do.

Some discussion between the skipper, the chief mate and myself and slings are lowered and two men jump aboard to lend a hand. The slings are led under the hull in the water and up around the outrigger. A hook is made fast and the ship's hoist pulls me out of the water and lands me on her deck all as pretty as a picture without a scratch to the paint. Beautiful.

The *Novelist* was bound to Dominica and had stevedores waiting so we took off at full speed for the island. Everyone on board was most kind and I had a shower and a drop of whiskey to ward off the chill and then breakfast. In the meantime I put right most of the things I could on *Cheers* and got her ready to lower back in the water when we arrived in Dominica. We were anchored off the island in about three hours after being picked up. The operation, from the time I was sighted until I was on the Novelist deck, took about an hour and a half.

No hitches putting the boat back in the water rightside up. The Chief Mate had it all figured out and she came upright easily and went over the side, again, with not a scratch to the paint. Took her in and laid alongside the Customs wharf with an anchor out to keep her off because of the constant surge. Both Customs and Immigration were very helpful and I had no trouble at all during the two days I spent there before getting the boat rerigged and taking off again for St Croix.

I appointed Mr. Joseph, of Rose & Co., to act as my agent in Dominica in order to speed things up and he was very good about doing whatever I wanted. I left a number of things in his office to dry out and took most of the other things into the customs shed where they furnished me with a locker. The sails and my sleeping bag as well as a cushion or two and some odds and ends I put in the backyard of one of the lads who stayed aboard to look after the boat. I hired two and one was there or nearby all the time. Things were a bit messy and I spent two nights in the Fort Young Hotel while rerigging.

The story according to Tom Follett

I lost a few things in the capsize exercise but nothing of much importance. One water jug floated away unnoticed and one cushion. A few cans of food disappeared plus a flashlight, a drinking cup and my sextant box. Fortunately, my sextant was heavier than water and it stayed in the boat although it rattled around in the bilge all night and didn't benefit from the treatment. Still -- it was put right again in Miami and I got hold of another box from Dick Newick to put me back in the navigation business again. My stove floated away and I didn't mourn its loss. For many years I have used a primus and have always thought highly of them. Still do. But *Cheers* was not the boat for a primus. Not much rolling or pitching but plenty of quick jerky motion which made cooking on a primus practically impossible. Solved that problem with a Sterno 'Sea Swing' stove.

I had taken along a Zenith transistor radio with a DF loop and this spent the night in the salt water. As soon as I got to Dominica I turned it over to a radio technician for cleaning and he soaked it in fresh water followed with a good cleaning with carbon tetrachloride. Wouldn't work though and I made the trip to England and back with a new one.

One steering rod was bent a little and was easily put right in Dominica and some slides were lost from the sails but not enough to worry me much. Other than that -- everything was OK except for the mess inside which my two hired crew managed to clean up somewhat.

Tried to call Dick Newick with the news but it took me the better part of a day and a half to get a phone call through to St Croix. I did make it eventually and let him know the trouble so he could start thinking about a modification to take care of the capsize question.

Took off from Roseau, Dominica on the morning of the 8th February bound for St Croix. Boat rerigged but in a filthy condition which I fixed as soon as I got out to sea a way. Usual light wind in the lee of the island and it took me most of the day to work my way out into some breeze. Not a lot of wind around Saba the next day and I used my no.1 jib (drifter) for a few hours. By midnight I was off the east end of St Croix and picked up a mooring in the harbor about 0200 hours on the 10th February.

Dick and I went out that same day to see if we could do a capsize at sea but, again, the wind was light and, even with the drifter up and sailing with the outrigger to windward, we couldn't lay her over. The next day we made a trip to St Thomas in *Cheers* and stopped at Hassel Island where we discussed a modification with Dave Dana and Ian Major. Then back to St Croix the same day for a good fast round trip. The remaining jib halyard block carried away on this trip and that took care of the light stuff we thought we could get away with. Some properly rugged blocks and fitting went up before I set out for England later on.

The next day, 12th February, we capsized the boat near the beach to check on heeling angles and then hauled her out to start modifying her. I took off for Miami to await developments.

The major modification, required as a result of the capsize, was the addition of a blister (or, perhaps 'sponson' is better) to the windward hull as high up as possible with sufficient buoyancy to prevent the masts from rolling right down to the water. This worked very well although 150 lbs of extra weight were added which neither Dick nor I were very happy with. The blister added nothing much to the appearance of the boat and it wasn't useable for stowage being rather flimsy but it fulfilled its function well enough although I don't recall ever heeling over enough to need it again.

A few other modifications were made while the boat was out of the water but these were mostly in the nature of shelves here and there to simplify stowage. The compass mounting problem was solved but we later had to augment it with another compass in England because of the difficulty reading the thing going backward.

Our compass was a cheap little job often used in automobiles. Fairly well damped and with easily read numbers but it was an 'aircraft' type as far as reading is concerned and this takes a bit of getting used to after getting used to the traditional ship type compass. One steers the lubber line opposite to the desired direction in a compass of this type.

Steering the lubber line opposite to the desired direction is bad enough especially on a dark night. But, if the boat is going backward relative to the mounting position, one would read SW (for example) if the heading were NE. Try that for size after making a tack (changing direction with *Cheers*) on a dark and stormy night. Wow! We were forced to mount two compasses so I could at least read one always in a forward direction. But this was after we were in England.

As well as the requirements for modifications I managed to get some good speed checks on the shakedown cruise plus all the information I needed on stores and water.

Hard on the wind for a period of nineteen hours with only the foresail up for twelve of those hours and the jib for only about half an hour checked out at 8.2 knots. Wind speed variable between 15 and 25 knots. I thought this was passable. A broad reach under foresail and mizzen with a 20 to 25 knot breeze checked out at 10.4 knots. The sea was rough for this one and I was a little disappointed at the figures. Seemed much faster at the time but, perhaps, it was because of the rough sea. Always seems faster then somehow. Two broad reach runs in a moderately rough sea with winds between 28 and 30 knots, now and then dropping off to 20, checked at 13.3 and 14 knots. My small Jib was up for these runs along with the foresail and mizzen giving me a substantial increase in speed. Then, another run hard on the wind with only the foresail and mizzen in a rough sea with winds from 20 to 25 knots checked out at 8.7 knots.

I reckoned, from this data, that I could do a twenty-four hour average of 10 knots without much trouble given a decent breeze and I figured this was good enough, to give us a good chance in the race provided the committee let us in.

After I got back to Miami I wrote the Yacht Club in England telling the Race Committee about the capsize and about what we were doing to correct the little difficulty. A reply a short time later was not encouraging but we decided to carry on and hope that sailing to England would sway the committee in our favor.

I had written a letter to my wife while in Dominica mentioning the capsize but I got back to St Croix before she received it. Another letter from St Croix arrived first so she didn't know about the contretemps until I was back on dry land. She was a bit annoyed and thought I was crazy to slosh about in a boat that was capsizeable. However, I assured her that Dick had everything under control and future capsizes would be nothing more than thrilling little adventures as we surfed madly down the faces of breaking seas dipping our sponson in now and then and bobbing upright to go merrily about our business.

Other people in Miami told me why the whole thing would never work. Plenty of advice on how to go about taking care of the capsize question most of which boiled down to never leaving the harbor. 'Illegitimus non carborundum' expresses (in Latin) my thoughts on the subject. It's great to be a linguist.

Dick kept me informed by letter and telegram about progress on the modifications and tests and I went back to St Croix on the 25th March confident that everything had been taken care of. A capsize to windward (getting caught aback) now posed no great threat primarily because of the sponson but also because of a very simple and effective sheet release mechanism. It would only work on the foresail and, I'm sorry to say, I didn't have a chance to test it in severe conditions. I suppose I really did have the chance on the way to England and on the trip back during the race but didn't feel like it then. Too cold. I prefer to do my testing, where a capsize might be involved, in warm water and under a warm sun just in case anything goes wrong. I did check the sheet release in mild conditions while in the Caribbean and it worked well enough then.

The mechanism was nothing more than cleats set athwartships near the foresail sheet blocks plus a short length of line with a loop in one end.

Haul in the foresail sheet until the sail is trimmed. Take the small length of line and drop the loop over the windward part of the cleat and run the other end around the boom of line to the same tension as the sheet and make fast on the boom. Release the sheet. The small piece of line is now the sheet and is holding the sail in trim. Boat gets caught aback and the loop slips off the cleat and the sail is free. Works every time. The mizzen would still be sheeted in but would not ordinarily be enough to tip the outrigger up in the air.

Undoubtedly one can think of conditions where both the sponson and the foresail sheet release mechanism would be insufficient security. Mizzen being enough to roll the boat up on the sponson for example. The sponson, being fairly flimsy, breaks up. Far as I'm concerned, let those who can imagine conditions like that worry about them.

The new blister didn't look too bad and I decided I might as well take off for England after another short cruise. This cruise was only for two days and I left St Croix on 27th March with the intention of stopping in St Thomas on the way back to get Manfred to take care of some leech flutter in the sails and to do some work on the fabric hatch cover.

The first night out, after a good sail with nothing wrong, I anchored in Coral Bay, St John's island. Unfortunately, I dropped my anchor in fairly deep water and it wrapped itself around a coral head during the night. I was unable to dive deep enough to free it the next morning and had to cut the line leaving me without an anchor since I carried only one to save weight.

Went over to St Thomas in squally weather and had to beat my way in the harbor. Plenty of space to do this but I still gave myself a good workout getting up off Hassel Island so I could run into the cove down wind. Plenty of mangroves at the end to cushion the crash in case I couldn't stop but I had spotted a mooring buoy as I went by and decided to pick it up and then call for Manfred to come and get me in his dinghy. Eased along into the cove under bare poles going at a fairly good speed. Picked up the mooring. Nothing on the other end. Oh joy! Oh rapture! Head for the mangroves Follett me lad.

A group in a Boston Whaler happened to be around inspecting me and offered to take a line and this saved me an ignominious ride into the mangrove roots. Turned out to be Bill Higgins with some friends over to have a look at his competition. Bill had *Axel Heyst*, an Angus Primrose design built in England, and she was entered in the Single-Handed Transatlantic Race and was due to depart St Thomas for England via Bermuda in a few days. In fact, about the same day I planned to take off in *Cheers*. Bill had a look around and, later in the day, I went aboard *Axel Heyst*. She was a beauty and, I'm sorry to say, did not compete in the race after all. I think she would have been a lot of competition.

Manfred got busy right away on the sails and the fabric top for the hatch and I went over to the town to see some friends. Planned to spend the night on my old boat *Ballymoss* which I had sold a few years ago and which had recently been resold to a friend of mine from New York. He was aboard and we had dinner together but I went back to *Cheers* for the night since the wind had piped up and the cove was at the leeward end of the harbor and I thought *Cheers* might need some extra weight to keep her from leaping out of the water the way the sea was being kicked up.

I made arrangements with Bill Kaye (the new owner of my ex-boat) to ride back to St Croix with me the next day and, after a passably miserable night listening to the howling wind and wondering how long it would be before I parted my dock lines, we took off the next morning. Manfred had the sails fixed up and the hatch cover was OK and we got Dick Avery to give us a tow out of the cove. Set the sails in the harbor and off we went with an entourage following in power boats. Good breeze and we chugged our way back to St Croix in about 3 1/2 hours under foresail, mizzen and no. 2 jib averaging about ten knots.

15. Another shot taken during early trials, showing large light weather foresail. Photo Fritz Henle.
16. This close-up taken during early trials, shows the cockpit layout and the netting very clearly. *Newick*

17. *Cheers* showing her paces during trials before the anti-dive plates and sponson were fitted. Photo Fritz Henle

Chapter two

St Croix to Gosport

The next day I loaded stores and took care of last minute odds and ends and was ready to leave on 31st March. Took a short sail out of harbor in the afternoon to see if everything was still OK and it was and *Cheers* and I were ready to hit the trail. Dashed off a letter to the yacht club in England telling them I was on the way and would see them in about a month for a chat about entering the race.

I had come to the conclusion that the following sample menu would be enough to keep me going and in good health:

> Breakfast -- small tin of fruit juice or, if cold weather, some cocoa. Oatmeal twice a week with some canned milk.
> Lunch -- One sandwich as long as the bread held out plus a can of beer. Sardines or tuna fish if no bread.
> Supper -- Half a can of meat stew mixed with half a can of vegetables plus a can of beer.

This worked fine and I lost only a little weight on the trip. The stores didn't take up much space and weight was kept to a minimum. I took along ten gallons of water although I had, at first, planned to take five only. As it turned out I used only two gallons. A couple of bottles of whiskey came in handy when the weather turned cool and a few cans of fruit served as a special treat now and then when I thought the diet needed a bit of variation. I had a little dried fruit and some nuts to munch on at night.

Two 'hurricane' lamps and five gallons of kerosene provided me with some heat after I got far enough north to need it. Not really sufficient but enough to keep ice from forming inside the cabin. Bit smelly and slightly conducive to seasickness but not very much trouble

Project Cheers

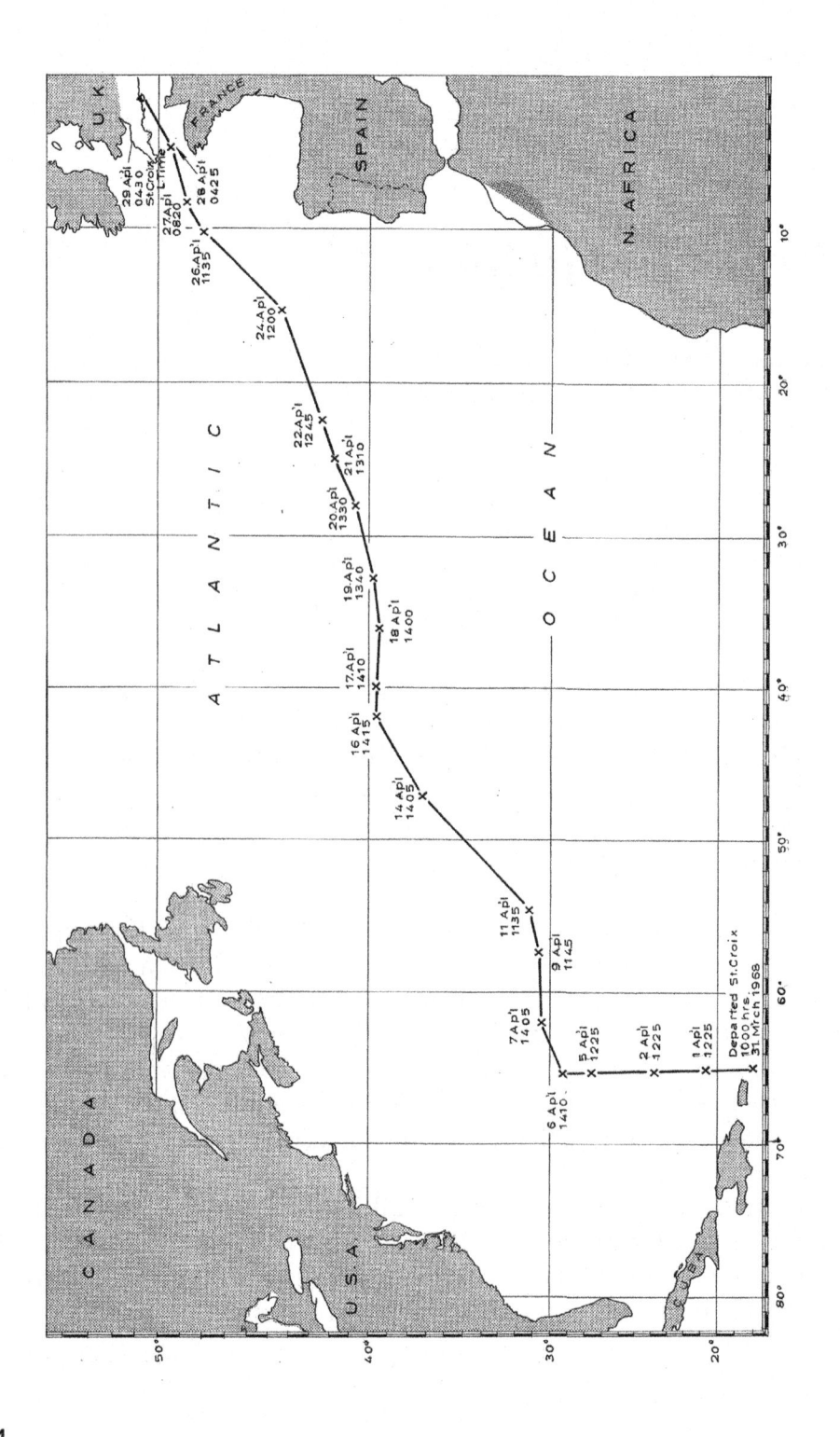

and taking up only a small space. Lots of warm clothing. Navigation equipment, including another transistor radio with DF loop, some books and crossword puzzles and a few odds and ends of spare parts. Plenty of space for stowage and room left over in the cabin for a game of tennis.

Providencia, Dick's power boat, loaded with farewell wishers and photographers towed me out of the harbor about 1100 hours on 31st March and I was on my way to England via Bermuda if the winds were right. Direct if not. Lots of people on the quay waving adieu. All very nice and exciting. Good breeze. Set the sails at the harbor entrance (exit this time) and took off like a scalded cat leaving *Providencia* behind. By 1400 hours I had passed through the northern string of islands between St Thomas and St John's and was on my way into the Atlantic.

Destination -- Gosport, England. This is on the English Channel very near the Navy town of Portsmouth and close to the Isle of Wight. Why Gosport? Because Dick Eames' yacht *Andiamo* is there at Camper and Nicholsons and he has offered the use of same as our tender until the race starts.

This yacht of Dick Eames' is an ex-German police launch about 70 ft LOA (single screw), which he had bought in Germany and had fitted out as a yacht at Camper and Nicholsons. Rather a nice job as a yacht with plenty of accommodation and quite good looking. Long and slim with a low profile and a business-like look about her. Not at all like the usual twin screw piece of junk one sees on the waters these days.

Also, Gosport would give us a chance to get the lay of the land before barging into Plymouth to beard the lion (race committee) in his den. A coat of paint wouldn't hurt and any other chores could be taken care of in an unhurried manner we hoped. As it turned out -- a coat of paint was just about all the boat needed. That plus a beefing up of some anti-nose dive planes we had put on in St Croix and a suit of racing sails from the Ted Hood factory in Lymington and we were ready for the race. In fact, I'd have been happy to start off the day after arrival after taking on a few stores except for the short stay in England. I like the place and like to prolong my residence there as much as possible. This was one of the reasons for taking off from St Croix so early.

A trip from the tropics to England during April offers a few problems not met with later on in the season. The crew hates to go

Project Cheers

north too fast without plenty of heat in the boat. Blood is thin you know: skin sensitive to fog; that sort of thing. On the other hand, one needs to go north to get out of the Trade winds and into the westerlies. The Trades don't often last much north of the 28th parallel but then the Horse latitudes must be reckoned with and it generally pays one to get up about 38 to 40 degrees north as soon as possible to be reasonably sure of some west wind. Can't go too close to the Portuguese coast either before heading up toward the higher latitudes. Northerly winds there blow fairly hard and it's a job trying to beat against them. What to do? Stay warm as long as possible. Pick up the west wind as soon as possible.

I thought I might as well start out for Bermuda and stick around there for a few days and leave with a nice westerly breeze behind my back. Probably carry this all the way into the English Channel. You are indeed a dreamer Follett!

Wind was NE leaving the Virgin Islands and I headed off for Bermuda right enough but with the prospect of not being able to lay the Island on one tack. For seven days I kept *Cheers* hard on the wind and found myself being washed off slightly to the west of Bermuda. This put me up only as far north as the 30th parallel. Then a few hours of westerly wind followed by a breeze out of the NNE let me head off in an easterly direction. So I forgot Bermuda and set a course for England direct.

With the exception of a few hours now and then I was hard on the wind all the way to the Azores which I passed fairly closely. That is; I went past Corvo (the most north westerly of the islands) leaving it to starboard about twenty miles distant. Didn't see it because it was night when I was abeam the island and rain was falling rapidly making visibility a bit dim. In general, I sort of wandered along inching my way north as slowly as possible until the 39th-40th parallels. Then eastward to the 30th meridian and, from there, a pretty straight shot into the English Channel with a fair wind all the way.

Practically always wind. That was the beauty part of this trip. Calmed a couple of times but only for a few hours. Mostly the wind was over ten knots and usually it was blowing me along as fast as I cared to go. Two gales -- both from a fair direction, one lasting about ten hours and then dying off to about 15 knots of wind in the space of about

The story according to Tom Follett

half an hour. The other blowing about 55 knots for a couple of days. Kicked up a nice sea and I had a good ride under bare poles with the boat as comfortable as my Coconut Grove apartment. More so in fact. No traffic noise outside my bedroom window. These two gales were north and east of the Azores and blew me in the right direction both times.

On 7th April, not far to the southeast of Bermuda, about sunrise, a ship passed me heading off to the east. Weather was fine and I was coasting along under foresail and mizzen with the no. 2 jib pulling nicely. Ship gets up ahead about half a mile and turns around. No doubt the mate on watch had called the skipper and reported a most odd looking object which appeared to be some sort of a sail boat. Back they came and made a circle around me and then the *SS Sonto Amaro* went on her way. Where bound? Italy maybe.

My worst fears were realized on this trip and it did turn cold very rapidly after leaving the 30th parallel. Up until then I had been enjoying a daily bath and a bit of sunshine while reclining in the net. But then the sky turned a sickly grey, the water a melancholy puce and my corpse a ghastly, grim and deathly white. Spent my time working crossword puzzles in my little nest or reading detective stories or memorising poetry or working out positions or eating or sleeping but, definitely, not bathing. I did sponge off a time or two when the situation became desperate but, oh, what misery!

The anti-nose-dive planes we had put on in St Croix were some help on this trip. In fact they got a very good workout. But they only postponed the danger of pitchpoling. Oddly enough it wasn't the wind that caused me trouble. It was the sea. North of the Azores I had a very nice run for several hours with the wind getting up to about 40 knots but without much sea running and my bows had no tendency to bury. But, as soon as the sea began to build up above about 7 or 8 ft, trouble would arise and I'd have to shorten sail. With a big sea running (over 8 ft) I'd have to shorten down very often even with the wind only about 20 to 25 knots. This, of course, with a considerable sacrifice in speed.

I doubt that *Cheers* would capsize to leeward even under severe conditions. Too much weight in the weather hull. Too much buoyancy in the lee hull and the rig not big enough to roll it over. But pitch-poling is rather different and this is a problem. I've never had this happen to me and don't particularly want to even though it might be exciting. The masts would, very probably, break off in a pitchpole and the boat would come to rest 180 degrees out of phase with the ocean. Truly an unhappy situation with but small chance for a cheerful ending to the story.

Steerage was never any problem in particular. There were a couple of combinations of wind and sail which made life difficult but these were easily taken care of by altering the sail. Usually a reduction, I must admit, with a consequent reduction in speed but this didn't often happen.

When things began to get clammy I kept my two kerosene lamps burning in the cabin all the time and the inside temperature was liveable. A horrible smell but I soon got used to that. The snag was condensation. There was already a problem without the lamps. They made it worse and water poured off the cabin sides flooding my bunk and keeping everything nice and damp. Could have thrown away all my fresh water north of 40 degrees of latitude and been quite happy sopping it up with a sponge from the interior of my solar still. Finally started to sleep in my oilskins which isn't a bad system once you get used to the feeling.

Didn't have any problem with navigation on the trip. Weather was usually overcast but the sun would appear now and then long enough for me to grab a quick sight. Stars were no good unless it was flat calm. Too much motion on the boat to bring one down to the horizon. The sun was bad enough but I figured an accuracy of about three miles which suited me. Before I left St Croix, Red Stolle told me about a system called 'HO 249' which is a set of sight reduction tables. I had always used my own system which required nothing more than a slide rule or a set of trig. tables but HO 249 looked pretty good and I bought a couple of volumes. One to take me from the equator to 39 degrees and the other from 40 to 60 degrees. I didn't worry about going north of the Arctic Circle.

I've been wasting my time all these years! HO 249 is so simple! Worked out a system where I don't worry about DR at all. A latitude is necessary now and then since one can't be too far away on that but I work backward from HO 249 to figure out an assumed longitude. Apply corrections then and the job is done.

The story according to Tom Follett

Only time I had any difficulty at all was just before entering the English Channel. No sights to amount to anything for about three days. But my transistor radio picked up the Ploneis Consol station and I eased into the Channel on bearing from him plus later bearings from Round Island and Ushant. Hit the Ushant Light (no damage) on course and on time. A little radio like that is quite handy. Takes up very little space and is useful for bearings in bad weather. Not really bang on for accuracy of course but, if one takes this into consideration, there is no difficulty.

While still a good thousand miles out from England I picked up the BBC on 200 kcs. and got some good jazz to listen to as well as shipping forecasts and news. Later on I could pick up the Home Service on the broadcast band for a source of nearly continuous entertainment. Can't think why some British don't like the BBC. Best system in the world I reckon. Not that I've heard radio all over the world but I have listened here and there and been pretty much disgusted. The only hope in the USA, for example, is the odd FM station one finds around a few of the large cities. But the British really have something worth while in the BBC. The French have a good system too I suppose but they talk too much. I prefer the sound of music to that of the human voice even though the French language is rather pleasant.

Enough about radio. I could carry on like this for a long time. Would you like to hear my views on government?

From the Azores to England. Lousy weather. Fair wind but lousy weather. Expected nothing better really. Fog. Rain. Cold. Sky overcast. Condensation leaking down my neck. No bath. No suns rays from the Holy heavens beaming down on my pale form. Heavy seas. Wind force 6 one minute and force 3 the next. How come they do it? How come the British and the French and the Dutch and all those people in that part of the world go to sea on yachts ? Ugh!

I ran into the English Channel with a nice depression breathing down my neck. I had been running off under bare poles for a couple of days before a 55 knot breeze with the barometer not much below normal. On 26th April the wind began to moderate a little and I managed to get a reefed foresail on and, about that time, made my first contact with the Ploneis Consol station. The sun came out and I gradually set more sail as the seas dropped and the wind became more

Project Cheers

pleasant. The weather was cold but I was fairly snug in my cabin and quite happy with life. Barometer got up to about 29.70 which would be cause for alarm in the West Indies but which I considered fairly normal for these parts.

Early morning on the 27th I looked at the barometer and it said '29.51' and I thought it was joking. Not at all! Down and up (mostly down) it went until it reached a low of 29.31 at about noon on 28th April while I sat around wondering when the hurricane would hit. The BBC shipping forecast would mutter something about force 9 behind me from time to time and I'd stand by with one hand on the sheets and the other on a life jacket but nothing much came of it all, I picked up a maximum of about force 7 between Plymouth and Portland Bill (from the right direction) but that was all and the weather was generally better than it had been previously ever since the Azores. Scared the wits out of me though. I'm not used to seeing the barometer get so low unless a howling gale is blowing around my ears.

No sleep going up the Channel. Shipping in abundance and, near the Channel Islands, fishing boats out the ears. Never saw so much traffic. Weather not all that good but the fisherman don't give a damn. Let it blow. Let it rain. Drag in them fish man. Had I dozed off for two seconds I'd have been wrapped up in a fishing net and hauled off to France for exhibition in a museum. Most of the boats were French. English had more sense than to be fishing in weather like that.

Even after I arrived at Gosport, the barometer stayed low but nothing much happened. The weather was stinking by West Indian standards but, apparently, quite normal for this neck of the woods. In St Croix they begin to evacuate the island as soon as the barometer drops below 30.00 but, in England, the barometer drops to 29.00 with people swimming off the beaches and yachts happily bobbing about in the 20 ft seas.

Did I say I had a fair wind from the Azores to Gosport? A lie! Wind came out of the east when I got to Portland Bill (maybe Anvil Point) and I had to struggle the rest of the way. Couldn't even lay on St Catherine's Point on one tack. Didn't want to slosh about in the Solent at night so went around the Isle of Wight as far as the Nab Tower and then on in to Gosport. Old England looked good to me as I rounded St Catherine's

The story according to Tom Follett

Point just after dawn on the 29th April. My wife and I used to live in England and it looked just like home.

Drifted into Gosport Harbor and there's Henry Chamberlain with a couple of friends in the Camper and Nicholson launch to give me a tow into the wharf. So ends the trip. Customs on the way. A bed and a bath await at the local hotel (*Andiamo* still on the slip) and a good dinner that is in the offing.

A nice voyage in spite of the cold. About 4,200 miles in 28 1/2 days for an average of about 1,000 miles a week. Just cruising. Not bad. Newick and Morris; I reckon we have a boat that might win the race.

Spent two nights in the Angelsey Hotel in Gosport until *Andiamo* went into the water. Henry Chamberlain and Annie Rice treated me to a champagne dinner the first night after I caught up on some lost sleep during the afternoon and Henry made arrangements with the yard to pull me out of the water the next day.

In the meantime, Cynthia and Ian Major had come over to England to spend a couple of months. I rang them and they came down to Gosport the next day for a reunion bringing with them the good news that *Cheers* was now provisionally accepted for the single-handed race.

We got *Cheers* out of the water and I sent in my films for development. Films? Ah, yes. I forgot about that.

Had dinner one night, at my apartment in Coconut Grove, with Woody Broun and his wife and Bud Lamoreaux. Woody does sports interviews for a CBS Television program and Bud Lamoreaux is the producer and they were in Miami Beach doing a job on some football players.

Conversation somehow got around to the Single-Handed Transatlantic Race. This is sport. The Broun interview program is sport. Maybe CBS might have a go. If CBS does do an interview after the race it might be nice to have some first hand film. Why not take a cine camera along on the boat and take some pictures? It wouldn't hurt to have them even though they're never used. I'm reluctant knowing nothing at all about cameras in general and cine cameras in particular but, according to Bud, these things are easy to use. He was right.

Jim Morris picked up a camera on the way to St Croix via New York and I took it along with me on the trip to England and back again on the race. It was indeed foolproof. All I did was point it and press the button and beautiful films were the result.

The film was developed in London at the CBS factory and my wife and I were invited to a showing. When I saw the result I was quite happily surprised and began to dream about a career as chief cameraman in the motion picture industry (offices in Rome and Hollywood) or, at least, as photographer for one of the big picture magazines with films of shattering emotional impact. So far, no one has replied to my job application but I'm expecting a phone call any minute. All I need is one of those CBS cameras and I can't miss.

Turned out CBS did do an interview after the race and some of my films were shown on TV. OK so it was only a couple of milliseconds. That's more than the average man in the street can say even after he's spent a fortune with Eastman & Co.

My wife came over to England on 3rd May along with Jim and Tootie Morris and Dick Newick. Pat Newick was to come over later on. Dick Eames had got us rooms at the Savoy and had laid on chauffeur driven Rolls Royces and we spent a couple of days at our ease in London. Like that Savoy. Love them Royces. Going to get me a job peddling heroin to high school kids so I can retire and live in the manner to which I have now become accustomed. Gosport, London, Lyminton, Plymouth. Delightful! Nothing much to do on the boat. Camper and Nicholsons taking care of it very well. Sorry I didn't come over a month earlier.

A telegram from Capt Shaw of the Royal Western Yacht Club offering congratulations on the fast passage over was most welcome and it somewhat confirmed the word from Ian Major that we would be allowed to enter the race. Not long before the newspaper reporters found us and soon we were in the English news. TV and radio people came around. Interviews going on all the time. Lots of fun with the news and radio and TV people being nice to know and a pleasure to talk with.

One fly in the ointment. Woke up one morning and had a sore foot. Thought I might have sprained my ankle somehow. Got worse. Someone diagnosed gout. Ian Major, who has had gout, said no. Sigh of relief. Someone else said arthritis. Maybe rheumatism. Maybe cancer of the pancreas. Could be the eustachian tube is plugged up. Blondie

The story according to Tom Follett

Hassler gave me a copper bangle. Only thing that did any good was for me to stay in bed. But I didn't come to England to stay in bed so, as soon as I could bear weight on the foot, I'd be off to London. Then, back to bed. Up and down. I never did get in good shape until after I left on the race. This worried my cohorts a bit and I had plenty advice about going to the doctor and what not but I managed to fend it all off confident that it was nothing more than a broken ankle that would heal eventually. Two days after the race began I could have walked across the USA which only goes to prove the saying; 'never go to a doctor unless you are foaming at the mouth'.

The day after I arrived in Gosport I called Bunty King at the Ted Hood factory in Lymington and let him know I was in and would like a set of racing sails. Bunty was good enough to let me have the sails in about two weeks so we could try them out on the trip from Gosport to Plymouth. A good job they were too being about half the weight of those we had brought with us from the Virgin Islands.

It was nice in Gosport for a couple of weeks. Not the weather, of course, but just being there and visiting some of the people we knew when we lived in England. I rather hated to leave even though the race promised to be interesting. England looked good to me after an absence of eight years and I thought; to hell with the bad weather. This is a nice place to stay. Why don't I go back? Well -- I reckon my blood's too thin now. Like that Miami heat.

Jim Morris and I sailed on *Cheers* in the Virgin Islands and we both knew it's no boat for more than one man on an extended trip but we decided that both of us would take her around to Plymouth. If the wind was light. *Andiamo* would give us a tow. If there was a breeze we could make it before things got too cramped. Neither of us reckoned it would be as cold as it was. We nearly froze and the wind was fair. Had it been foul we'd really have been in bad shape.

With two people in the cabin on *Cheers* things are a bit tight. One man has to stay in the bunk and can't see what's going on and the other sits on the seat and cooks soup. To reverse the order is a problem. Best, really, to have both men go outside. Then, back into the cabin in reverse order. But, if it's cold and wet, better to try some contortions.

Project Cheers

We had a lovely sail down the Solent but J. Morris saw only the water dripping off the cabin sides. Next time Jim -- we'll cut a porthole in the side for you.

Henry Chamberlain towed us out of the harbor about 1400 hours on the afternoon of 18th May. We had a BBC photographer aboard to get pictures of me working and we were to put him off in the *Andiamo* tender and they were to take him ashore before heading off for Cowes. We had tentatively planned to rendezvous around Yarmouth and hoped to anchor there to have supper aboard *Andiamo* before taking off on the overnight run to Plymouth. My wife and Tootie Morris were on *Andiamo* and Pat and Dick Newick were driving Dick Eames' car to Plymouth.

Wind was nearly flat calm when we left Gosport. Soon as we were clear of the harbor the wind began to pipe up and squalls came from here and there. We reached back and forth across the Solent a few times for the benefit of the cameraman and then put him off in the tender. Kept on reaching back and forth in a good breeze to permit pictures to be taken from *Andiamo* but we finally had to take off for Plymouth by ourselves when *Andiamo* got the tender line in her prop and had to be towed into Cowes to get it loose.

Arrangements had been made with Mr Beken in Cowes to come out and take some professional photos as we went by and we arrived there at 1630 hours just about the time agreed upon. Mr Beken was there in his motor boat and got some good pictures. Overcast weather though so no nice cloud formations in the background. The breeze was light then and we had a fair tide and were moving nicely under foresail, mizzen and no. 2 jib. Before we got to the Needles it was cold and the wind was increasing and, with the fair tide, we were flying along at a good rate.

We made a nice passage to Plymouth arriving there the next morning just after daylight. Wind got up to about 25 knots during the night and it was a beautiful sail in the lee most of the time since the wind was out of the north. But cold!! Jim and I drank soup until I thought we'd pop and the kerosene lamps were going full blast to ward off the chill. Coldest part of the trip that little voyage.

Sailed into Plymouth in bright sunshine. Still cold. Dropped the anchor after coming in behind *Myth of Malham* who had left the Needles about the same time we were there and who passed us as we were becalmed near the breakwater at the entrance to Plymouth Harbour. I was too cold then to put up a jib and we were just drifting along. Dragged our anchor down the line a way before it caught and we slept a while until a launch came along with Capt Shaw aboard to give us a tow into the Millbay Docks. Once again we had to cut the anchor line since it was fouled too badly to get loose and I didn't fancy diving for it in that cold water. We really use up a lot of anchors on old *Cheers*.

Went into the Millbay Docks (no tide worries there. One goes in through a lock at near high tide) and tied up and met the people at the yacht club and got squared away in a hotel and waited for *Andiamo* to come in. Newicks showed up in the afternoon and *Andiamo* arrived in the evening and, after she tied up in Millbay Docks, we went alongside her and remained there until the start of the race.

I enjoyed meeting the people at the Yacht Club and they were a very nice lot in spite of not wanting to let us in the race. I could understand their trouble and didn't blame them too much. They have a hard job to do and I don't envy them at all. Altogether, they did very well and the race was most efficiently organized. Not the easiest thing in the world to get people from half a dozen different countries together in one place at a given time and have them available when necessary not to mention the difficulty of passing on the seaworthiness of a yacht someone thinks is the last word in seagoing elegance and who has spent perhaps his last shilling on fitting it out for the race. One would have to be hard hearted indeed to say 'sorry amigo'. On the other hand. there is the possibility of an unseaworthy yacht coming to grief with consequent loss of life. This is bad enough but there is always the voice of doom saying; 'I told you so. There ought to be a law against single-handed sailing.'

Receptions, parties, interviews. Meeting the other contestants. Always something interesting going on. Time passed too quickly in Plymouth and it was soon departure day.

The favorite sport in Plymouth, while waiting for the race to begin, was checking the competition and listening to the remarks of bystanders. Admiring some of the very fast looking yachts and, in some cases, admiring the nerve of those planning to put to sea in some rather horrible pieces of junk. 'Look, Doreen, some clot thinks he's going to cross the Atlantic in that! He must be out of his mind.' Easy there mate

-- that there is *Cheers* -- I'll put a bomb in your pocket if you don't shut up.

Shortly after we arrived in Plymouth we took the *Andiamo* tender and nipped over to Mashford's yard and there we saw *Voortrekker* on the slip. Here was a fast looking boat indeed and she was a beauty. Bruce Dalling, the driver, was busy enough without us bugging him so we let him alone and contented ourselves with an inspection of the exterior. I immediately wrote him down as potential trouble if I expected to win the race and, as it turned out, he was very difficult to get along with indeed, beating me into Newport by several hours. I dreamed one night, shortly before the race, that five yachts came in within about half an hour of each other at the finish line with me, of course, the winner and *Voortrekker* behind me by one minute and 20 seconds. Just goes to show how dreams aren't to be relied on any more.

Two very fast yachts (three, in fact) failed to turn up at the Millbay Docks until rather late and we didn't have much of a chance to look over the winner *Sir Thomas Lipton* or a big French entry called *Raph* or Eric Tabarly's big trimaran. These were all formidable looking contenders. *Raph* and the big trimaran had to give up the race or I should probably have had trouble placing even third with *Cheers* the weather being what it was.

I had managed to get £20 down on myself to win at 25 to 1 with the prospect of having £500 to spend when I returned to England to pick up the first prize. However, the way things looked a couple of days before the start with the heavy competition; I didn't start then to count my winnings. I figured that, given a reasonable amount of wind with some close reaching breezes now and then, I could do the trip in twenty to twenty-one days and I thought this would be enough to take the big yachts like *Sir Thomas Lipton*, *Voortrekker* and *Raph*, but Tabarly was a horse of another color and I figured him to give me a beating if the weather was light provided he had no trouble with his boat which was only recently launched.

Strikes and political hobbledehoy really loused up things for a lot of the contestants this last race. Alex Carrozzo had a hell of a time getting his big catamaran to Plymouth and he was sadly hammering in nails, even as the race started, trying to put her together.

The story according to Tom Follett

It wasn't a strike of workers that delayed *Sir Thomas Lipton*. Poor guy got struck by a hovercraft off Cowes and was bashed about a bit. Didn't seem to affect his performance though and he breezed across the Atlantic and into Newport in rather good time to win first place.

I wrote down some of the big catamarans and trimarans as being good competition if we had reaching breezes. Tabarly's boat first as long as the wind was light enough but I reckoned his outriggers not buoyant enough for heavy weather. Experience counts rather heavily in multi-hulls and I put Bill Howell with his *Golden Cockerel* high on the list of people to beat. *Ocean Highlander*, another catamaran, looked good and Martin Minter-Kemp with his multi-hull experience promised some difficulty with *Galicia Girl*.

I don't know about the rest of the field but my trip was made in light headwinds most of the way. Flat calms now and then. One ten or twelve hour blow from the NE (but then it blew so hard I had to get all sail off) and about 24 hours of NE wind at the end to wash me into Newport but, again, blowing so hard most of the time that I was either well reefed or under bare poles most of the time. Took me twenty-seven days and a few minutes for the trip and I came in third which made me £20 or £500 poorer depending upon which way you look at it. Oh, I did have some good runs all the way over so it wasn't all slow but the overall effect was of one big drifting match.

Project Cheers

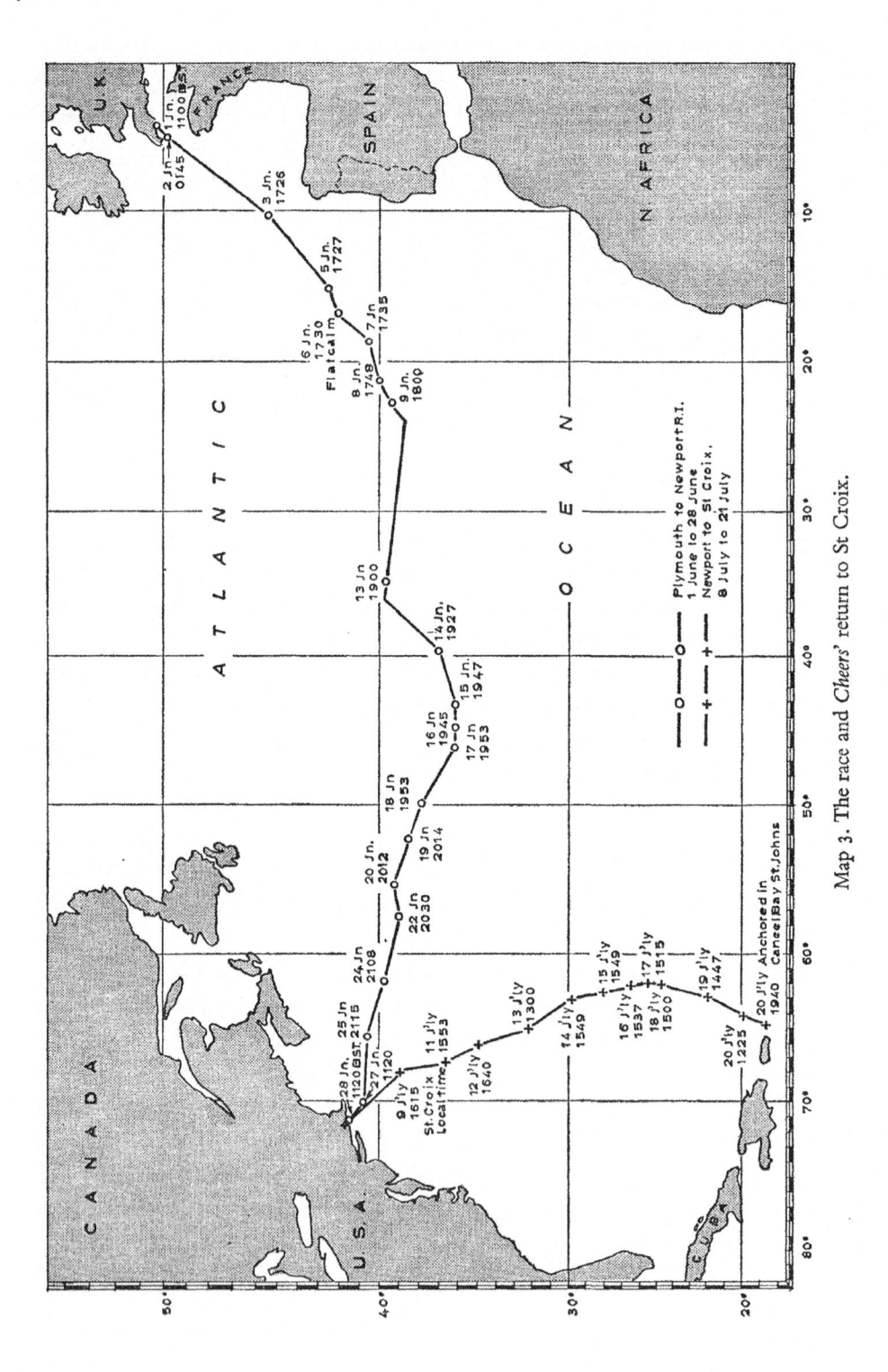

Map 3. The race and *Cheers'* return to St Croix.

The story according to Tom Follett

Chapter three

The race and some subsequent musings

Newick gave me a tow out of the Millbay Docks with the *Andiamo* tender about 0830 and I picked up a mooring outside to take care of last minute odds and ends. The boat needed to be cleaned up a bit and some stowage problems needed seeing to. Jim Morris and Rod MacAlpine-Downie were in the tender and jumped aboard to lend a hand scrubbing down while I tended to the stowage and got the sails rigged. Dick buzzed off to get petrol (gas to you Yanks) so he'd be ready to tow me out into the assembly area when the time came. Of course, being England, it started to rain.

I had thought to be all nicely stowed and ready to go a good day in advance but I forgot about people giving me things. Poor old Newick looked at all the stuff I was taking along and nearly collapsed. 'Look at the ruddy waterline! This is a race, you idiot, not a confounded pleasure cruise. What about all those chocolate bars? You'll never be able to eat them all. Let me have some.' Have no fear Newick my son. You'll be able to follow the Follett trail out of the harbor and across the Atlantic by all the stuff going over the side. I gave him one chocolate bar.

Time grows short. All passengers and cleaners up ashore! Tender stand by! Kindly give me a tow into the assembly area. Done. Drifting with the tide. Ten minute gun. Up foresail and mizzen. Five minute gun. Up no. 1 jib (drifter). Over the line not long after the gun for a passable attempt at a racing start. Not much wind. What there is comes from the west. Rain. Hundreds of thousands (maybe even millions) of spectators. Rather a difficult problem keeping them clear since there is no law in England reserving a given patch of water for the exclusive use of any particular yacht. Coast Guard can't say 'I'll clap you in prison if

Project Cheers

you don't get out of the way' so one has to rely on the good sense of the spectators and, this race with plenty of help from the Royal Marines, there was no trouble.

Cheers began to slowly move up through the fleet. Very light breeze, just enough to keep the no. 1 jib drawing and provide steerage way. Had it been a foul tide we'd probably have drifted back to the Millbay Docks. Came up on *Myth of Mallham*. Rev. Pakenham on *Rob Roy* paddling away with a couple of huge sweeps shouts to Noel Bevan as he passes by; 'Just wanted to say I was ahead of *Myth* at least once during the race.'

Going along close to Bob Wingate on *Zeevalk*. Checked his compass for him on a couple of headings. Joan de Kat making good time in *Yaksha*, comes close by to break the monotony.

Late in the afternoon, just before sunset, I could count ten yachts all fairly well bunched up with the wind still light and variable. By this time I had given myself a good tacking workout as the wind shifted here and there. Finally, just about dark, a nice breeze came out of the north and I began to move. That's the last I saw of any contestant until I arrived in Newport and saw *Sir Thomas Lipton* and *Voortrekker* waiting at the dock.

The breeze was quite good the first few days although from the WNW mostly and I went off in a southwesterly direction either close hauled or close reaching. Later on the breeze became light -- very often from about 1 to 5 knots for days at a time -- and still from the WNW varying a bit now and then into the north and I carried on through the northern part of the Azores all the way down to the 36th parallel before coming about on the port tack and taking a northwesterly course for Newport.

By the end of the second week, in spite of the light winds, I congratulated myself on being in a good position and on having covered a respectable distance. I was then very nearly 2,000 miles out from Plymouth at 36-32N lat. and 43-24W long. I figured then about 1,400 miles to go to Newport and although it was practically flat calm at the time, I counted on some southwesterly breeze to wash me into the finish line on a close reach. *Cheers* likes a close reach and I thought that, with a little luck, I could do the 1,400 miles in a week or eight days.

I had been getting some pretty good runs over twenty-four hour periods all along but this would be only in spurts and then I'd sit around sunning myself in the net and swimming alongside the boat while the wind whistled through the rigging at 1 or 2 knots. This usually with the no. 1 jib sheeted in as tight as I could get it and still make headway. One twenty-four hour period I reeled off close to 250 miles for a better than 10 knot average but it cost me two degrees to the south which I could ill afford at the time.

I planned, soon after the start, to go no further south than the 39th parallel but the WNW breeze didn't agree and, in order to get some close reaching runs, it was necessary to bear off well to the south. I don't think *Cheers* is a boat to pinch when the wind is more than about 10 knots. Better off then, I believe, to bear off and let her move rather than try for the shorter distance. Anyway, in the North Atlantic, the winds are often variable enough to make it well worth while for even a ballasted hull yacht to avoid sailing too hard on the wind. What you lose in latitude one day you'll likely earn back the next. Not so this race but probably just an odd year for weather.

I thought I could do the 1,400 miles in a week to eight days! Rave on MacDuff. Things got no better. Worse is more like it. Took me a fortnight to get to Newport rather than one week. In the meantime I whistled. I scratched on the mast with my finger-nails. I wept. I poured out a libation of my precious whiskey. A bit stingily I'll admit. Found a child huddled in the outrigger trying to get a free ride to the USA ('emigrating' he said) and I cut his throat. Genuflected toward Mecca. Said 'omni, padmi, mani, hum'. Nothing worked.

This is what comes of going to sea in a sail boat. Made an old man of me, this race did, and well before my time too.

On 20th June I was at 39-30N and 55-32W and my plan was to hang on to that latitude until I reached the 61st meridian. This, I hoped, would keep me south of the Gulf Stream until I could cross it at a favorable point. I heard about Brenda on 22nd June and, since hurricanes have a mind of their own, I thought it might be prudent to toddle off in the direction of Halifax, Nova Scotia in case things began to get sticky (or, rather, windy). This put me in the Gulf Stream a little before I planned and might have caused some delay. Hard to tell.

Project Cheers

I do know there was no improvement in the Stream although the water was warm. Wind was fluky and it poured rain most of the time. Sea would be kicked up and then the wind would die out leaving me slatting about and cursing the whole business. The Gulf Stream is a wicked place if one is trying to make headway against it and my case was no exception. I lost a lot of time fiddling about in its clutches. And all I was trying to do was get out of it. Not make headway.

Probably my imagination but it seemed to me I was in the Gulf Stream longer than I should have been. At any rate, the water was warm well up toward Halifax and I could picture myself being washed back to the eastward at a horrible clip. I guess it was good for my peace of mind that sights were non-existent at the time and I didn't really know where I was for a couple of days. Otherwise I should probably have cut my own throat in an effort to appease the Gods.

My vow to Newick, before leaving on the race, that my trail could be followed by the things I threw overboard, was kept. Kept a bit too well and I nearly froze as a result but the boat grew lighter and faster after each throwaway session. Early on in the trip I got rid of five gallons of water -- I had taken on ten -- plus a good supply of tinned food. Like a half wit I didn't use the fresh water for a bath. Pitched it out first then wondered why I didn't think about bathing with the stuff. Oh, well! One can't think of everything you know. Later on, as I found my supplies holding out well enough, more tinned food went over the side as well as anything I could think of that wasn't being used. At the time it was nice and warm for a change and I threw away my two heating lamps plus all the kerosene (paraffin to you English types). Shortly afterward my sea boots packed up and they went over the side too. About this time I crossed the Gulf Stream and it turned cold. God-it was cold! Cold and clammy.

So now wet feet all the time. Nothing but hot soup and cocoa to keep the chill away. Last of the whiskey used up trying to appease that lousy Poseidon. I'll get even with him. Next time I sacrifice a child I'll keep the blood for myself and pour tomato sauce over the side.

I nearly went mad in the Gulf of Maine. Sitting about in a flat calm 150 miles southeast of Boston. Cold and overcast. Barometer down. Boston radio telling about 30 knots of breeze in the harbor. Me with nothing. Finally picked up some wind early in the morning of 27th

The story according to Tom Follett

June. Also fog. Also fishing boats. Like the English Channel. Fishing boats all over the place. No sleep for Follett. Not sure of my position but know I'm in the vicinity of George's Bank. Can pick up the 'unreliable' sector of Nantucket station and Nantucket Consol station and Nantucket Shoals Lightship comes in faintly for a bearing of sorts.

Wind picks up rapidly but the fishing boats don't go away. Like the French, they don't care anything about bad weather. Fortunately, the increasing wind blows some of the fog away and I can breathe for a change. Wind out of the NE (how nice!) and I'm really screaming along but the seas are building up fast and it's time to reef down. By the time I sighted the lightship at 1620 hours (British Time) I was down to a reefed foresail and really making time. Then the home stretch to Newport with bare poles part of the time. Reefed foresail now and then. Reefed foresail and reefed mizzen when there was a lull. Nasty sea. Nasty weather. Bearings OK from Buzzard's Bay entrance.

Chugging along under a reefed foresail and three New Bedford fishing trawlers passed me by. Bit of a lull when they're about half a mile ahead. Set a reefed mizzen with the reefed foresail and the boat takes off like a bird. I pass the fishermen in about an hour and leave them behind like they were anchored. Most fun I had the whole trip although I was looking out for a pitchpole at any time. Bit later-down to bare poles again.

Weather got worse. Rain squalls so thick you could slice them and make sandwiches. Thought I'd get a lee from Martha's Vineyard but the sea didn't seem to want to moderate at all.

Picked up the Brenton Reef light about midnight still in heavy rain and tried a tacking exercise to see how it went. Badly. Tough job in squally weather with a pitch black night. Brenton Reef a lee shore for me so -- the hell with it. Hove to under reefed foresail to wait for daylight. Little did I know that Newick, Morris and Co. (Ltd.) were out in a powerboat waiting to give me a tow after I crossed the line. They stooged about between Brenton Reef light and the whistle buoy until about two o'clock in the morning before they went home while I happily dozed off now and then. Seems I had been reported from Nantucket Shoals Lightship and Dick had it figured out when I'd arrive. Had I known it I'd have gone on in over the finish line but c'est la vie.

Project Cheers

Crossed the finish line just after daylight on 28th June for a total time of 27 days and 20 minutes for the trip.

Coast guard came out to give me a tow and Jim and Dick were aboard. Probably had a worse night than mine. My wife was waiting on the dock (how did she manage to get up so early in the morning??) with the rest of the gang plus all the children and we tied up alongside at the Port O'Call Marina for an end to a nice slow race. Boat looking as good as it did the day I left Plymouth. Nothing broken. Something to be said for simplicity on a yacht in spite of what the stock boat salesmen tell you about radio transmitters, radars, deep freezes and heads to accommodate eight people at the same time. Keep 'em simple. That's my motto. Then you can be miserable at sea without worrying about your electronics going on the fritz.

I made plenty of sail changes on the race and plenty of tacks. But there were really only two major tacks as far as I'm concerned. The starboard tack leaving England which I held for more than two weeks and the port tack to the finish line. I dithered about on one tack or another from time to time but only because of fluky winds and, in general, I wouldn't hold anything but my main tack for more than a very short time. Sail changes kept me busy enough. The drifter pulled nicely in light air but, to be really close hauled, it was often necessary to use the no. 2 jib without enough wind to justify it. Then too, it was often prudent to douse a jib before it was time during the night owing to the difficulty in getting the thing off in a breeze.

I think we could have used a taller rig in this race to good advantage. Not only bigger jibs because I doubt that I could handle anything more but the foresail and mizzen were easy enough and another 6 to 8 ft on the hoists would have given us a good boost in the light air we usually had. In this case, perhaps, two sets of reef points rather than one.

Perhaps it's because I'm more cautious now after capsizing once, but I don't think there was ever a time either going over to England or coming back in the race or, later on, on the way back to St Croix when I was in danger of being caught aback and tipped over to the sponson line. Not that it would have made much difference if I had tipped except for dislodging stowed material.

The story according to Tom Follett

The motion, as I have said before, is a bit jerky but the boat is always on an even keel and there's no trouble keeping things upright on the table. With no decking other than the net, there is no tendency to pound into the seas except now and then when hard on the wind when the forward end leaps out of the water and the hull hits back away from the sharp entrance at the bows. In general, I would say this is a most comfortable boat with a nice easy motion. The jerkiness is no bother at all once you get used to it. Not so easy to write legibly but that's the only drawback. I'd much rather be reaching along in a good breeze in *Cheers* than heeled over on my ear in a ballasted hull yacht.

Newport was delightful and so were the people. Turned warm the day after I arrived and the weather was good from then on until I left with *Cheers* for the Virgin Islands. Port O'Call Marina was the HQ and a group was always gathered there trying to find out news of the next arrival. Mrs. Bevan was down every day peering out into the haze for a glimpse of *Myth of Malham* but she had a long wait. Noel Bevan was becalmed in the Gulf of Maine and in, Block Island Sound and he arrived No. 8 about a week after *Cheers*.

John Groser, of the *Observer*, was staying at Port O'Call and we'd down a pink gin or two and then tell him how we wanted him to write his articles for the paper. 'Heavy on the details of personal heroism there Groser me lad.' The Black Pearl (a gem of a pub) had some delicious clam chowder and thick roast beef sandwiches to keep us going and was within a few feet of the marina. A beer to wash down the good food. Pleasant company. They picked a good place to start the race and Newport, Rhode Island was a nice spot for the finish.

The Ida Lewis Yacht Club was handling the finish of the race and Mr. Thomas was always available for anything that might be needed. Jack Odling-Smee, from the Royal Western Yacht Club, was in Newport when I arrived and he stayed on for a few days to greet some of the other contestants before going back home to heave a sigh of relief and get ready for the next race in four years. Mr. Thomas and his wife had come to England before the race started and were on hand at the skippers meeting to answer questions about Newport and the finish arrangements. Another example of the excellent organisation.

Time now for a few general remarks and observations.

There is an argument that it is unseamanlike to sail single handed and, I think, that is a valid enough idea. Not having a lookout at all times is not the best way to cruise about. On the other hand, the average single hander is on a small boat (small enough, that is, for him to handle himself although this past race seemed to indicate that pretty hefty craft now come under the single-handed category) and, if he crashes into someone or someone crashes into him, he is likely to be the one to suffer. The chances of hitting another single-hander are fairly slim. More likely it'll be a freighter or a tanker. Single-hander goes to the bottom. Too bad! But nothing much happens to the tanker. In fact, he probably doesn't even know he's hit something.

Single handling is also a bit unseamanlike because of a chance of a knockdown while the crew sleeps. On the average ballasted hull boat this is no particular problem unless an unusual situation arises and water pours in through open ports and hatches and the boat sinks. Doesn't happen often enough to worry about really. A multi-hull is a bit different though and I don't think single handing in these machines is something for the novice. Best to have three or four hours practice first.

A multi-hull is a capsizeable craft any way you look at it in spite of what some designers, and a good many salesmen, have to say about it. Some of them will sink after a capsize. Others will not depending on what's inside but, unless a person is very lucky, a capsize at sea very often means goodbye crew. Still -- no particular strain if the crew is small and only a limited number of people care one way or the other.

So -- for my money -- viva single-handed sailing. On a ballasted hull boat if you like, but on a multi-hull also if you're the type.

There's always a hue and cry when something happens and someone has to be rescued at sea. There are people who will weep about the expense of it all and cry about the waste of manpower being diverted from important activities to pull some guy off a sinking yacht. But, what the hell, all this is one way to enjoy life. Better than sitting at home quaffing a whiskey and soda. Gets the blood circulating. I don't advocate people pushing off in cracker boxes with the expectation that the world is going to exert every effort in their behalf if they get into trouble. I don't think anyone who goes to sea in a yacht has a right to 'expect' anything in the way of assistance. Pay your money and take your chances. But don't stay home. And if you get into trouble and

The story according to Tom Follett

some cheerful soul wants to help you out -- jolly good. If a rescue ship fails to turn up at the last minute and you become a resident of D. Jones' Locker the world will still continue in its orbit around the sun.

One hears a lot about multi-hulls vs. ballasted hull yachts these days. Which one is better? Depends on what you like, it seems to me. I like the feeling of complete control at all times (well! ... most times) while sailing an easily handled, ballasted hull yacht through a crowded anchorage. I like the accommodation that can be easily fitted into a 40-ft single hull without lousing it up. Put the same accommodation into a catamaran or a trimaran of equal length and, chances are, you end up with a piece of junk. But I don't like beating to windward or even reaching in a good breeze in the average 'monhull'. I'll take a multihull then every time.

I don't care about the difference in safety between the two types. I'd just as soon be safe if it's no trouble, but it's the least of my considerations when going to sea on a yacht. If I want to be safe I'll stay home and keep off the highways. Won't eat any leafy vegetables when in Mexico and pull the covers over my head during lightening storms. One thing I can say for sure and that is I'd be fairly content with a clunker of a monohull if I couldn't afford anything better and it looked decent, but I could never last more than a few days on what I consider to be a poorly designed multi-hull. With this type: if you ain't got speed you ain't got nuthin'.

Enough of that. Like to hear my views on government? Some other time perhaps.

After a few days at the Port O'Call Marina we took *Cheers* over and put her on a mooring at the Ida Lewis Yacht Club so there'd be room for some of the other contestants. Shoved off from there on the 8th July bound for St Croix. Nice day. A breeze from the SW. Sunshine. Fair tide. Two days later; under bare poles, now and then. Reefed foresail from time to time. Blowing like the devil! But not for long. After it was over I had a good run down to Bermuda and passed the island about ten miles off to the west. Fair wind then so kept on going.

South of Bermuda the wind died off quite light but still fair. It worked its way around to almost due north and I poled the drifter out opposite to the foresail and mizzen and had a nice run dead before the wind. Very comfortable. Held course bang on all the time. Spent my time in the net soaking up sun and enjoying life, thankful not to be in a race where every last ounce of speed would count.

Picked up the trade winds rather far to the south -- around 24-30N latitude - -and was east of the meridian of Bermuda at the time so had a beautiful reach on into the Virgin Islands. Arrived at St John's just after dark on 20th July and went into Caneel Bay and dropped the hook for the night. (Didn't lose my anchor this time.) About 12 1/2 days from Newport. Not bad. Not good either, but not bad considering the wind south of Bermuda.

On the way down from Bermuda I kept a good radio lookout for hurricanes but nothing was reported. Mostly excellent weather all the way with no really flat calms to worry about.

On into St Croix early on the morning of 21st July and there was Dick Newick on the quay. Tied up to complete a round trip of about 9,000 miles in a sailing time of 68 days. Ah, *Cheers*, you did well indeed even if you only came in third on the race. You were a first place boat. Trouble is, you only had a third place skipper.

Dick and I took off all the gear and, last I saw of *Cheers*, she lay on a mooring in Christiansted Harbor ready to head for shelter when the hurricane season gets into high gear. And so ends my part of the story. But, before I go to bed, let me reiterate a few points and, perhaps, add some I've forgotten.

Late thoughts on Cheers

The idea of a single-handed race across the Atlantic intrigued me a couple of years ago. After doing the race once, I'm intrigued even more although I still don't know why. Maybe I do know why but I can't pin down any reasons that make sense or, at least, I can't pin down any reasons that would make sense to anyone other than myself. Certainly not 'because it's there'. I like heated rooms and feather beds, clothes of silk and shoes of fancy leather. I like wine served in good crystal, well cooked food on fine china and a fair young maid standing by telling me what a fine chap I am. I do not like the North Atlantic Ocean. You figure it out.

I'm looking forward to 1972 and the next race. I'm convinced I can win with a boat like *Cheers* given a reasonable break in the weather provided, of course, that guys like Tabarly are unlucky with their monstrous multi-hulls. Maybe a taller rig and a couple of roller furling jibs. Some slight alterations in the sheet and halyard leads. A lighter sponson perhaps. Not many changes.

Will I enter? Will it be in *Cheers*? I don't know. But if I do and if it is in *Cheers* I'll have another 20 quid riding on her noses to show a clean pair of heels to the rest of the pack.

Handling *Cheers* was never an easy task although she would steer herself nicely once trimmed. Working to windward was a hard job. Long tacks not too bad provided there was plenty of time to rest in between but a beat up a narrow channel would be no pleasure. Even the Solent, for example, would be too narrow for comfort with the wind from dead ahead.

To take care of *Cheers* in a rising gale was comparatively easy. Compared, that is to the average ballasted hull yacht. The only difficulty was being down in the cabin with the boat off the wind when things could get a bit rough before being noticeable. But that's pretty much the case in any yacht.

Going to windward, sail would generally have to be reduced down to a foresail by the time the wind was up to about 30 knots. At much more than that a reef would have to be tied in but then *Cheers* would be quite comfortable in winds to 45 knots especially in a regular sea. She would make 4 or 5 knots hard on the wind like this in a fairly easy manner.

Off the wind, as I mentioned before, the danger of pitchpoling controlled the amount of sail to be carried and this was a function of the height of the seas more than anything else.

Nearly always I'd be down to a no. 3 jib with the wind 15 knots or more and this would come off when it blew harder than about 20 knots. Not because I couldn't comfortably carry a no. 3 jib even in a 30 knot blow on -- say -- a broad reach but because I felt I'd lose the thing trying to get it off in winds over 20 knots. Jibs were set flying and were very hard to control even under moderate conditions.

Of course, things look much different at night when it's windy and it's probable that I frequently reduced sail before I needed to after dark. The danger of pitchpoling at night was greater than during daylight since there was no particular change in the feel of the boat when the bows started to dig in. On a trimaran I can somehow sense a need for sail reduction at night but not so on *Cheers*.

Reefing the foresail and mizzen was much easier, I think, than reefing any other boat. Even a trimaran. Steadier platform than any trimaran I've been on so far. I used a lacing around the boom and through grommets in the sail in the conventional manner and would douse all sail and let the yacht drift to do the necessary work. It took me about ten minutes per sail but *Cheers* was quite steady with all sail off. The booms were steady with the endless sheets pulled tight in both directions and the topping lifts (doing double duty as jib halyards) set up. I'd steady the booms off at right angles to the hulls and stand about in the net while tying in the reefs feeling very secure. Past experiences trying to reef down a monohull yacht, with the boat rolling around and me hanging on with both hands and tying in the points with my toes, makes me thankful for a steady base of operations like *Cheers*.

I wonder what would happen with *Cheers* if a mast were lost? It wouldn't be a serious matter to lose a dagger board although it would be quite troublesome. The boards are slightly round on one side and flat on the other in order to provide some lift to windward and, since the rudders are an integral part of the boards, they are not really interchangeable. But they will fit in either slot and one board could easily be made to do the job both ways. A bit heavy and awkward to carry but possible for one man to change ends with them. I don't know about losing a mast. One could go along on one tack well enough with the remaining mast acting as a foremast but using it as a mizzen would be difficult unless well off the wind.

I think a jury rig could be easily set up on *Cheers* if part of a broken mast were saved. A short mast could set up on a connecting member close to the weather hull with adequate shrouds and stays and, quite likely, some control to windward could be realised. I'm not sure I'd like to have a go at it myself but I believe it could be done if necessary.

What about *Cheers* compared to other types? How about future boats of similar design? At the moment, my feeling is that *Cheers* strictly a racing machine with little chance of becoming a popular type except to a limited audience.

I like the motion of *Cheers* compared to a trimaran or a ballasted hull yacht. Not sure about a catamaran not having much experience with the type. I'd like to try *Golden Cockerel* or *Ocean Highlander* for comparison. But *Cheers* is not a cruising boat nor do I think the type suitable for cruising because of the difficulty in getting sufficient accommodation into a moderately sized boat. If she isn't suitable for cruising she should be suitable for day sailing or weekending but, I think, she's too difficult to handle in crowded conditions for even this.

An outboard engine would help (be a nuisance because of weight and stowage problems) to pick up a mooring and to get to windward in a narrow channel or to maneuver in a crowded anchorage and *Cheers* would be a lot of fun in the West Indies or the Bahamas for two people. In the tropics where it's warm and two people could stay out of the cabin most of the time without freezing there might be possibilities. With some practice, two people should be able to cut the tacking time down to about ten seconds or slightly less. Still not good compared with a 40-ft. trimaran but passable.

Carry substantial liability insurance with you when you take *Cheers* out for a sail. This goes for anything like her at the present stage of the design.

Project Cheers

Part Three

Design and Construction

Project Cheers

18. Close-up of *Cheers* in action during trials. Photo Fritz Henle.
19. A close fetch at high speed during trials. Photo Fritz Henle

20. Sponson and anti-dive plates fitted. Photo Newick.
21. A close-up of one of the anti-dive plates. Photo Fritz Henle

Chapter one

The idea is born

For years single-hulled craft had pleased me greatly. Then in 1957 I designed and built the 40 ft catamaran *Ay Ay* for my day charter business in St Croix. She did her job well, accommodating up to twenty guests, but was not intended to be particularly fast. In 1960 the trimaran configuration claimed my attention, starting with *Trine*, followed at intervals of about two years by *Lark*, *Trice* and *Charterer*.

The multi-hull concept is exciting, but too many multi-hulls do not capitalise on their wonderful ability to sail fast. This is often due to an overload of gear and gadgets that are seldom used and often unusable. To me, comfort at sea means a two week passage as opposed to a four week passage, given adequate food, a dry berth plus room to navigate, eat, read, and work the ship. Comfort also means easy motion. Trimarans with deeply immersed outer hulls and heavy catamarans can have a snappy, short, quick roll in a beam sea. Ballasted craft often roll rhythmically and sail at a considerable angle of heel.

Offshore, the proa's potential interests me right now, but where maneuverability is important I like the trimaran. For short passages with a large group of people the catamaran is my choice. Yachtsmen who need a piano, deep freeze, radar and machine shop to go to sea should have a heavy, ballasted keel boat. Certainly no one type can be all things to all people.

Hydrofoils can give an impressive lift contributing to speed by either lessening displacement or decreasing heeling, but, like wing masts, they need more development before they will be practical offshore. The reason is sensitivity to the inevitable quick changes in angle of attack when a gust or big wave hits the craft. These quick changes cannot be anticipated or counteracted, so most of the theoretical advantage of foils and wing masts is dissipated in less than optimum conditions. Small craft in sheltered water are now using these

Project Cheers

sophistications; their experience will show us how to best use them at sea, in the future.

Meantime, the unknown qualities of the proa concept intrigued me since it seemed to offer the most performance potential of any configuration available today.

The chance to design something along these lines came when in mid-1966 I got a letter from my old friend John Goodwin in South Africa asking my opinion about the size and type of craft it might take to win the 1968 Single-Handed Transatlantic Race. We knew something about Lt Col H. G. Hasler's idea of the Single-Handed TransatlantIc Race -- a designers dream! Create anything, the one man crew would be the equalising factor, the big question being how large a boat one man could handle. The first Race in 1960 indicated that in sizes up to 40 ft at least, the larger the boat the better. Francis Chichester won that year in the largest craft racing. The 1964 race was convincingly won by French Navy Lt. Eric Tabarly in his 44 ft ketch, again the largest boat in the race.

Anyway John Goodwin knew my multi-hull enthusiasm was still strong. For his part he had plenty of ocean sailing experience. He had sailed his 25 ft Vertue *Speedwell of Hong Kong* over the Atlantic some twelve years previous and his solo record of 26 days stood for some years. Later he skippered *Stormvogel* for a year. Unfortunately by the time I had given his interesting request some thought and sent some sketches to South Africa John was already committed to an experimental 25-footer using many of Bernard Smith's fascinating ideas about buoyancy hydrofoils and wing-shaped rigid sails. He freely admitted, however, that these advanced concepts could not possibly be incorporated in a serious effort to win a 3,000-mile solo ocean race to windward without a great deal of time-consuming trial and error.

Thus I found myself thinking about the strange racer I had drawn wondering if some of her wild ideas shouldn't be tried even if John Goodwin couldn't build her just then. The original drawings showed a double hulled craft which I called a proa, even though the hulls were both the same size, like the usual catamaran, but with two vital differences, which made her a proa: she could be sailed in either direction and most of the weight would be carried in one hull.

Design and Construction

This was my first attempt at a proa design and early sketches reflected the influence of the traditional Pacific Island proas with a small outrigger always kept to windward of the main hull. These Pacific Island craft were sailed by several persons who scrambled back and forth on the connecting structure, using their weight to counter the tipping tendency of the wind in the sails. No solo crew would want to sit out on a sea-swept outrigger in the North Atlantic, so I had to look elsewhere for a means of making a proa stiff enough to carry her sail.

Thus the outrigger grew each time more weight was added to it. First came the stores, then the skipper himself, then the rig, followed by the daggerboards and finally even the rudders. By this time the two hulls were the same size and the only use for the now vacant lee hull was to provide buoyant stability and perhaps, if the wind came from the 'wrong' side, weight stability. Access to the lee hull, or 'ama' as the Pacific Islanders call their outrigger, was provided to give storage area in case it was necessary or if slightly more weight there might prove desirable. But, as any sailor knows, it is better to have weight to windward, and now all of our major weights were placed to windward.

Next came the question of how to sail her efficiently in either direction. Obviously the rig and underwater shape, would have to be the same at each end of the boat, which was achieved by a twin masted schooner rig and identical daggerboard-rudder units. The either-direction requirement takes much getting used to by traditionalists who are used to having firm and irrevocable bow, stern, port and starboard on their craft. But if the craft had to have the heavier hull always to windward on either tack the only way it could be done it would be to have bow and stern, port and starboard interchangeable. Sheet leads, boom clearances and duplicated gear on each end of the proa give many opportunities for ingenuity -- and headaches. Some questions were only answered by later events as we went along. To do otherwise would have frustrated me to the point where I probably would not have dared to start.

Accommodation for the skipper was not an early major concern, but obviously he had to eat, sleep, navigate and sail the craft for a few weeks if he were to win a transatlantic race. So, simple needs were provided for under the rounded deck of the main hull. Only in the plexiglass surrounded, canvas-topped cockpit would the skipper be

Project Cheers

able to stand erect, but at least he would have reasonable shelter at the helm.

After we heard that John Goodwin wouldn't be building what was then known as our Design Number 25, wife Pat could clearly see my growing interest in building and sailing the proa myself. It had suddenly become more than just another drawing to both of us and I got the very dear message that it was obvious to Pat that the Single-Handed Transatlantic Race was fascinating to read about, but only for other women's husbands to enter. I was pleased to know that she liked me, anyway.

To get the dream proa launched we needed a skipper to race her and funds to build her, probably the skipper being the most important. Just then Tom Follett sailed into Christiansted on a delivery job. We see Tom as he comes in with yachts to and from almost anyplace on delivery jobs. I had first met Tom on a cruise we took together from English Harbour, Antigua to Florida in his 23-ft sloop *Native Dancer*. In those days he was working as an electronics engineer, and, like most career-limited people, couldn't get as much time to sail as he wished. Tom had arranged to sail the boat north with a friend and I was invited along. It was a good cruise despite a two day calm off San Salvador and a nasty electric storm in the Gulf Stream. This voyage showed Tom to be an excellent shipmate, but a very light eater despite his powerful build. He provisioned the boat based on his own intake, which left us with nothing at all extra at the end of our trip.

We kept in touch and met again several years later when Tom and Priscilla arrived in a new 27-ft sloop *Ballymoss* also designed by Alan Buchanan and English built like her predecessor *Native Dancer*. The Newicks enjoyed the Folletts company and their quiet way of savoring life. Out of this visit came my wife Pat's skill with the guitar as Tom imparted much of his considerable knowledge of the instrument to my musical wife.

This was 1964, the year Charles Case and I launched *Trice*, the second trimaran we owned together. We expected great things of this 36 footer and dreamed about doing a little showing off with her - -say go along with the '64 Bermuda Race, starting behind and keeping clear of the official racers, just to see if we had as good a boat as we thought we did. We had passed everything then sailing in the Caribbean, so had to

Design and Construction

look further for competition. In the 1950s some west coast catamarans had passed the fleet of Honolulu racers to the cat sailors' considerable delight. The Bermuda Race is not a downhill sleigh ride like the West Coast Classic, so maybe we could give our trimaran a more meaningful test.

Off we went, pleased to hear in Bermuda on our way north that Arthur Piver in his 38-ft trimaran *Bird* had similar ideas after he realised that he couldn't make the second Single-Handed Transatlantic Race as he had planned. On *Trice* Tom Follett was again a great shipmate along with Rudy Thompson and St Clair Childs. We passed all but *Nina* and *Stormvogel* in a 145 boat race that was all to windward leaving Piver in his larger trimaran over twelve hours behind. We could almost hear a few old eyebrows being raised and see a few tired eyes opening a bit wider, so, aside from the fun we had, maybe that trip had some educational results too.

Another lesson learned about Tom on this voyage was that he is not what could be called a 'gung ho' racing type. He doesn't have to prove himself to anyone, so shuns 'unnecessary' trouble. The more competitive types aboard *Trice* gave him some good-natured kidding about his easy going nature.

When questioned in 1967 Tom admitted that he'd been vaguely thinking about the 1968 S.H.T.R. and certainly would be interested in sailing a fast proa if we could come up with one. We had a skipper.

Now for the hard part: the syndicate. Sailing friends are used to my enthusiasms and sometimes like to share them over a beer at the end of the day in a waterfront cafe, but to share the cost of making a dream come true -- that takes more than congenial talk! Jim Morris, whom we've known about ten years, gets to St Croix once or twice a year from Denver. In the summer of 1967 the Morris and Newick families were planning a month's cruise in our catamaran *Ay Ay* from St Croix to Grenada and as many of the islands in between as time allowed. Jim and wife Tootie had been on hand through the birth pangs of many of our previous craft, so naturally they heard about the latest dream soon after arriving for a vacation from the frozen north. Jim's first reaction was one of cautious warning that so many people in such a project might be more headaches than the actual boat itself. Granted, but how else could we raise the $10,000 I then naively thought would build and campaign the boat?

Within twenty-four hours Jim came back with the simple answer: 'Let me do it.' Just like that. All we had was a piece of paper with some lines and simple calculations on it. One friend said, 'Sure, I'll sail the thing, 3,000 miles alone.' Another friend says, 'Sure, I'll buy it.' With people expressing that kind of faith in me, thoughts of success were tempered by agonising moments when the load seemed extra large --- What would happen to Tom if the hulls broke apart, if she hit a large piece of driftwood at 15 knots, if she capsized ... How would Jim feel if the whole concept was impractical ... 'What if .. .' was to be a not uncommon thought in my mind for eighteen months, but I certainly did ask for it!

Jim had two firm conditions, typical of the man: We would go 'first class' all the way, cut no corners, use only the best materials, get the best professional advice if we needed it, and plan on winning. Anything that was going to soak up this much time and money should not be hindered by halfway measures. Secondly, our wives (admittedly more sane than we are) should be able to enter into the project with enthusiasm and feel a part of it. Indicative of the amateurism (in the best sense of the word) of us all is the fact that no one ever inquired about prizes offered in this race.

The drawing my friends saw was of a 40 ft equal hulled proa with asymmetric hulls, two equal 'wing masts' with fully battened sails, all weight possible in the weather hull where it would be most useful in counteracting the force of the wind in the sails. The rudders were small, near the ends of the weather hull, arranged to be cross-connected, both working at all times. Simple daggerboards were shown, each adjustable because the whole configuration was so new and different that the poor designer had to use these two variable boards as 'fudge factors', hoping to balance the lateral plane with the sail area in this manner. A windvane stearing gear, centrally mounted to windward was shown, but not with much conviction on my part. Several simple model linkages indicated that here was plenty of room for mistakes before we got what we wanted, if ever. Biggest headache about the windvane was wondering how often the rig would be caught aback, swinging the boom around far enough to the windward side to hit the vane. Early in the game Tom said that he believed she could be made to steer herself, so we might at least dispense with the steering vane until we checked her steering characteristics on trials. Fine with me -- that much sooner we could launch her!

Jim and I met with Tom in May to formalise the project. By this time further thought had changed the design in that the very sophisticated wing mast was discarded as was the asymmetry of the hulls. It seemed to me that the easy lines of a 40-ft hull only 27 inches wide could not be made asymmetric enough to affect windward performance. The daggerboards, very efficient hydrofoils, relatively deep in the water could have the section to give the most lift to windward for the least drag when sailing hard on the wind.

Early discussion had finalised our choice of wood as a material, mainly because cold molded plywood is still the lightest proven hull construction method. And light weight would be vital. Throughout design, building, and test phases the principal question asked about any proposed change or improvement would be, 'How much does it weigh?' Who ever heard of running a race with a heavy knapsack on one's shoulders? Just think of some nice little gadget -- maybe a radio telephone weighing 20 lb, which doesn't sound like much and might be a reassurance to have aboard. But it needs a battery, which needs a generator, which needs fuel, which needs a tank. Total perhaps 150 lb. Now try to imagine pushing an extra 150 lb of water out of the way of a boat for 3,000 miles all across an ocean!

Design is a series of compromises, balancing such desired factors as speed, stability, maneuverability, ease of handling, reliability, and comfort, keeping in mind the craft's intended use. One limiting factor in the design was the length of my shop, which only permitted about 40 ft to be built under cover. Width is a compromise between the stability required to carry the desired sail area, limited by the strength of the connecting structure and the fact that too stable a craft has a very quick, uncomfortable motion.

The rig required compromises between easy handling by one man and the 'power' required to realise the high speed potential of the easily driven hulls. The proper amount of sail area must be provided for wind from any direction at any force from mere zephyr to howling gale. Roller reefing booms that could swing more than 180° soaked up much of my time, but were discarded after the first sea trials as not being flexible enough.

Ordinary wire supported masts were not feasible since the masts were on the weather hull with no place to fasten shrouds to windward. We liked the simplicity of unstayed spars, but aside from the sophisticated modern Finn dinghy and rugged old fashioned fishing craft, there is little information available on the design of unstayed mast suitable for our needs. So we decided to play it safe with two extra strong, relatively short (30 ft overall) masts each carrying 165 sq ft in a boomed sail and capable of hoisting varying sized headsails to the masthead in light and moderate weather. Of course, the rig had to be symmetrical about the centerline for sailing in either direction.

Sloop rigs occupied much of my time in the early design stages but the strains on an unstayed single mast stepped amidships frightened me. Besides, I wanted the cockpit right amidships. So the schooner rig evolved. Stepping the unstayed masts that would be capable of supporting 500lbs at their tips 27 ft above the deck caused some engineering anxiety, as did anchoring the connecting structure into the hulls.

Steering gear had to be light and reliable. The original drawings showed interconnected rudders at each end of the craft, swinging through 360°. Strains calculated were considerable, so was the complicated linkage and the vulnerability to damage if the forward rudder struck driftwood at any speed. A novel modification that came early in the construction phase was to incorporate rudders into the aft edge of the daggerboards. Since the forward board would be always at least partially raised to balance the sails its rudder would be locked into the centerboard trunk or even be completely housed in it. Rudder area was small. The faster a boat goes the smaller the rudder needs to be, but I often questioned just how much area would be required to turn these two long hulls at low speed.

One advantage a proa has over other multi-hulls is that she is not required to come into the wind with enough inertia to carry her about on to the other tack after the wind in her sails has ceased to drive her. Thus, lightweight is no disadvantage and we could do with a smaller rudder and less 'rocker' to the keels which would give us more directional stability once on the desired course. This directional stability is vital to a single-hander who cannot be constantly at the helm. He needs a craft that will look after herself with a minimum of effort and attention.

Project Cheers

Chapter two

Cheers *is built*

These thoughts were playing tag in my head for the first half of 1967. Many materials were ordered in May. Hulls were to be three 1/8 in layers of diagonally laid up African mahogany veneer, resorcin glued, covered with polypropylene cloth and epoxy resin. Bulkheads were to be 12 mm mahogany ply glassed into place. They would support center board trunks, 'akas' (crossmembers between the hulls) and the mast steps as well. Ends of the hulls would be filled with polyurethane foam, solid within 5 ft of the ends. This would be good insurance against hitting a large piece of driftwood at high speeds. The 'akas' were to be laminated Sitka spruce with walls from 1 7/8 in to 1 ½ in thick, 8 ½ in high and 8 in wide.

Masts were to be the best available grade of clear Sitka spruce, hollow boxes with rounded corners, the sides tapering from 1 3/8 in at the butt to 5/8 in thick at the truck. Overall 6 ¾ in at the butt tapering to 3 ¾ in at the truck. These figures are how they finally ended up after we shaved about ¾ in from the walls in an effort to get the best combination of light weight and strength. Before starting to shave them down we sat 500 lb of boatbuilders at the tip, supporting the lowest 36 in as if it were in the boat. Deflection measured over two feet and the tip which didn't seem extreme but still we never again dared to load the tip with 500 lb. With 20-20 aftersight vision it still is hard to say whether or not we were over prudent in our design factors of safety. Nothing broke in 10,000 miles of sailing, so presumably everything was adequately strong. Also it is likely that most things were far too strong and hence excessively heavy. Some day it would be good to be able to build a replica of *Cheers* weighing perhaps a third less, then drive her in extreme conditions to see if these nebulous 'factors of safety' were excessive. But for *Cheers* with Tom offshore, racing to windward in the North Atlantic, the factors of safety couldn't be tampered with.

Project Cheers

The Single-Handed Transatlantic is a rugged race to windward in an area where gales are common. The winner would be the man with the boat that could be driven hardest under a wide variety of conditions. *Cheers'* size started at 40 ft, the length of our shop, but it turned out that we underestimated the monohull competition. Had we heard of Eric Taberly's trimaran early enough we might have been tempted to stretch our own effort, but we were too complacent about the large monohulls, about which we had heard rumors from across the ocean. We knew little about the boats against which we would be competing and proceeded with a simple faith that we were going to give Tom a vessel that could win.

Mental effort started to be translated into three dimensions in mid-June 1967. Walford Galloway is a young craftsman in wood, fiberglass and metal who has worked with me for several years. He had the skippers of our charter fleet to help him when they were not sailing and in addition we were lucky to have Bernard Rhodes sail into Christiansted one day. Bernard is a young Englishman who had designed and built his 22-ft trimaran *Klis* in which he sailed Trans-Atlantic breaking the solo record. Quite an accomplishment for one so young on a limited budget! His skills were immediately put to good use.

Actual drawings were minimal, more for myself than anything else, but Wally and Bernard soon had the lines translated into a 40-ft long strip planked 'plug' planked of ¾ in square redwood over frames spaced every two feet. One plug would do for both hulls. Only the decks were different. The planking was to have no framing except stem, keel, sheer clamp, and the few bulkheads necessary for bracing daggerboard trunks, 'akas' and mast steps. The first diagonal layer of flawless 1/8 in thick African mahogany went on quickly with just enough temporary nails to hold it in place. The 12 in wide strips needed very little fitting where they butted against each other, due to the extremely easy lines of our long hulls. The next layer went over the first at a 90° angle, fitted a few at a time then glued, using pressure from hundreds of nails driven through small squares of plywood, which made their removal after the glue dried (relatively) easy. These were often re-used several times and very soon Bernard coined the phrase 'dofor' for these little units. ('That will do for now.')

It was slow work, but not difficult and soon the hull was three layers thick with sharp outer stems flairing out the ends, well sanded and ready to be removed from the plug.

Any project needs a periodic sense of accomplishment to give the people doing the work a reason for the bit of extra effort that makes a big difference. Just sending over to the neighborhood bistro for a drink for all hands when the first hull came off the plug accented the sense of accomplishment. Despite a paper barrier between plug and hull the glue has seeped through in places, tenacious stuff, making it a bit of a struggle to remove the hull, but with some prying, banging and the proper language, off it came -- seemingly light as a feather. The Newick's bathroom scale, hastily commandeered, showed a weight of 145 lb after the inside was disc sanded. *Great*!

Weight was always on my mind. The original goal of 2,000 lb for the boat ready for sea seemed reasonable at that stage, but I should have known better. Only an optimist would rather dream new dreams than follow well-worn paths to known destinations. I dreamed of 2,000 lb ready for sea, 20 knots reaching, 10 knots to windward and an easily handled rig that wouldn't be a tyrant to Tom Follett, who would have to get the most out of it. Perhaps Dick Eames' description of his favorite four wheel vehicle is most apt. He says of his Mercedes SL 300 'This is a car you wear -- you don't just drive it.' *Cheers* with her tight accommodation and sparkling performance would be a boat for Tom to wear -- not sail, so I was continually mentally measuring Tom and his considerable ability, as the design and construction phases continued their overlapping progress.

Small modifications were few; fortunately, most of them took place in my head before Wally, Bernard and I had to alter work already completed. Being on the scene daily and doing some of the actual work myself plus conversation with Wally, Bernard, and the rest of the crew helped to minimise blunders that would otherwise have slowed us down. My enthusiasm was perhaps somewhat contagious, but our last major project, the 36-ft trimaran *Trice* had been so very successful that often my friends and fellow workers wondered why I was trying to improve on what they knew was a fast, easily handled boat that had amply proven itself. In my own mind it was obvious that a longer boat, with a better sail area to wetted surface ratio and a better sail area to weight ratio would have to be faster. Another consideration was the fact that the non-existent solid deck area on *Cheers* compared to the approximately 400 sq ft of deck of *Trice* would be a great safety factor in extremely bad weather when a light craft with considerable 'wing' area might either fly like a kite or be crushed by tons of falling water in a giant breaking sea.

Trice was a good boat in 1964, but the eternal optimist in me said that we should be able to do better in 1967 for solo offshore racing. Jim and Tom had diplomatic suggestions, but left the design decisions to me -- a show of faith that only time might justify.

Hull Number 2 went more quickly. The deck was laminated of three layers of 1/8 in plywood -- heavier than I wanted, like every other aspect of the design and construction. It was natural to think how sad it would be if the thing we were working on at the moment failed, so the boat gained weight as we progressed.

The humpbacked deck of the main hull had to be built, just like the hulls, with three layers of 1/8 in veneer laminated over a mould, but this time the mould was only 20 ft long and the two identical halves were joined in the middle to speed production. It was fun to be able to cut out the section where the cockpit would be located and flex the pieces removed, trying to imagine if our torture tests would ever be equalled -- or surpassed -- at sea. Torture tests on 12 mm plywood covered with both 4 oz polypropylene and 10 oz fiberglass each bedded in a special flexible epoxy resin proved to our satisfaction that the lighter nonflexible polypropylene would not shatter under extreme blows with an eight pound sledge to the extent that the fiberglass would. Good; another few pounds saved.

While the crew was finishing hulls and decks I started playing with a beautiful pile of clear spruce boards that were to be our spars and connecting cross members, ('akas'). These 'akas' had a high arch in my drawings. It is so easy to draw a pretty curve, but often quite another thing to translate it into three dimensional reality. To start with, we used a hydraulic jack on the ends of a fourteen foot length of 1 5/8 in thick spruce, holding the middle down with a prop to the roof of our shop. When we started raising the roof we suspected trouble. Not even soaking and prayers prevented a sickening split; once again Newick was too optimistic.

Design and Construction

Then came the trouble of laminating top and bottom of the 'akas' with two of 3/4 in thicknesses. Stronger, with considerable less built in stress, but more work. When done, each of the two laminated 'akas' had to support more than the total displacement of the craft even before being covered with a double layer of ten ounce fiberglass and epoxy resin. This sounded reasonable, but there were always nagging doubts back in my mind about shock loads and extreme conditions, so even before this stage had been reached I shipped my meager drawings over to friend Dave Dana in St Thomas, forty miles to the North. Dave, unlike me, has a fine technical education, which he has used to design many handsome vessels. I asked him to check the structure for weakness, and was relieved when his figures more or less reinforced mine.

Perhaps much of yacht design can today be called a science, but my feeling is that what we were attempting with our proa was more in the realm of art than science. At least, I didn't feel much like a scientist as I sat down with slide rule and a few simple formulae to try to arrive at some semi-educated guesses. Dave's figures were reassuring.

It was hard for me to get out of the office and into the shop, which was where my heart was, but Wally and Bernard needed a steady supply of materials and rough sketches of how to put them together; this kept me busy. At the age of forty-one I found that the eighteen hour work days that a new boat seemed to warrant ten or fifteen years ago were no longer practical. So, for a long time my letters to Tom and Jim predicted launching and trials in 'two more months'. Fortunately, they knew enough to discount my usual optimism.

Joining the hulls together permanently with the curved 'akas' was a real cut and try proposition; lots of cuts and many tries until we had each hull in the same horizontal plane and their vertical center lines parallel. The sequence of placing the twelve millimeter ply bulkheads each side of the 'akas' and glassing them in place with three layers of ten ounce cloth and epoxy resin before resorcinal glueing the 'akas' to the bulkheads necessitated some group discussions on the most practical methods. This accomplishment gave reason for another minor celebration and a boost to our morale.

Our shop building barely contained the craft, which frustrated attempts to get meaningful photos, or even to step back to admire our work. To picture the final visual effect of the structure needed considerable imagination. Sometimes she looked small to me, sometimes large.

We had our quota of visitors with the usual questions and comments. I was always interested in the thoughts of experienced seamen. One criticism that proved true was the comment of Arthur Connor who was *Trice's* first skipper; he thought that the bows were not buoyant enough. Even adding two inches more freeboard at the ends did not satisfy him. My aim was to minimise windage and make the hulls easy to drive through even rough water, thinking that the craft's extremely light weight and the unusually low center of effort of the sail plan would keep the bows high enough. Only the sea could show us the final answers.

Laminating the masts went well, thanks to use of friend Fletcher Pence's portable twelve inch planer, a masterpiece of German engineering, which made tapering the sides a practical proposition in our simple shop. We started with very strong masts thinking that they could always be cut down later -- very little science here! Not many modern seagoing craft have unstayed masts; still less do multi-hulls, with their considerable initial stability, so we left ourselves room for later adjustment. Just looking at our effort in the shop after they were initially shaped led me to reduce the wall thickness by ¼ in all around for a worthwhile saving in both weight and windage. I was hoping to get enough flexibility so that the spars would automatically flex enough to flatten the sails in strong winds. This desirable feature eluded me due to the necessity of providing enough strength for an adequate factor of safety to carry the load of the jibs right at the masthead where they imparted an enormous strain.

Hollow booms, slotted for the sails' boltropes, were made and then cut down as the masts had been. Their roller reefing goosenecks soaked up an inordinate amount of our time. I was inspired by a fitting that L. Francis Herreshoff had designed many years ago, which will some day probably be widely copied, but not on proas. The more than 180° flexibility required of a rig that must go in either direction frustrated all innovations. My original thought was to allow Tom to do almost everything, even reef, from the snug security of the cockpit, reasoning that if sail changes were quick and easy he would be more likely to keep the boat moving at her maximum speed as weather conditions changed. More over-optimism.

Dagger boards and rudders had by now been combined with the thought that if they did not work we could fairly easily revert to the separate rudders first drawn. Construction in welded aluminum was considered, but time was short and facilities for modification were not handy in St Croix. After harassing Jim and a Denver fabricator I simplified with fiberglassed wood done here: 1 5/8 in thick vertical grain douglas fir with a three layer ten ounce fiberglass covering. This construction had previously proven adequate on our 36-ft trimaran *Trice* with more sail area and center board area, but, the strains imposed by the built-in rudder of 1.6 square ft were somewhat of an unknown quantity. The problem of custom hardware procurement was given to Jim in Denver who came up with exactly what was ordered in stainless steel and aluminum with Tufnol or Micarta bearings. Beautiful functional jewelry for our girl!

Suddenly it was time to think about the cockpit structure, a net between the hulls, and a deck box in the lee of the main hull for stowage of spare line, light sails, and other gear. *Cheers* had purposely been given minimum stowage area with the idea that if there were large lockers they would almost surely fill up with 'essentials'. With good knowledge of Tom's definition of an, 'essential', (which coincides with my own), it seemed best to keep the storage areas small.

The 'hammock' net took shape on our living room floor with too much space between the two inch nylon webbing, light and strong, but not safe enough at sea. We finally doubled the number of webs leaving about three inch squares between them, which worked well.

The cockpit was important because here Tom would spend most of his time. Three-eights inch plexiglass screwed and bolted to corner posts and the deck structure made it quite strong and gave good visibility when seated at the helm. This was the only large opening in the whole structure, about 2 ft x 2 ½ ft. We expected flexing to take place here and tried to allow for it with strong framing. Access to the deck was provided for with removable boards on the lee side. The fabric canopy 'pram hood', as Bernard called it, was left for later.

Dutch built, heavy duty aluminum framed windows were let into the deck of the 'ama' (leeward hull) to give us water-tight access hatches to the stowage lockers there.

The object of our efforts had by now been named *Cheers*. She needed sails and a great many lesser gadgets to make her a seagoing vessel. I believed some well-known sailmakers' advertisements about their 'pioneering spirit' and 'research minded organisations' and wasted considerable postage before recognising Dave Dana's wisdom in suggesting that Manfred Dietrich in St Thomas would do a fine job, and was right on the scene for alterations, as required. Manfred worked closely with us and shared our enthusiasm, meeting every deadline.

Winches to handle the sails were unusually vital on this craft with one man doing all the work and having to do it going in either direction. We started with Barient and were glad we did. Blocks came from Gibb in England, light weight cleats from Wilcox Crittenden in Connecticut. A double acting Henderson bilge pump was connected to each hull. Running lights and other things not immediately necessary for the trials were put on lesser priority lists. Steering linkage for trials was a temporary affair to test questionable details. Sheets and halyards had to belay in several odd places until leads could be checked at sea.

Cheers even had her first simultaneous drinks of champagne and salt water without benefit of winches. Only seagoing experience could help us to place the hardware wisely. We had no precedents to help us with our backward proa.

Design and Construction

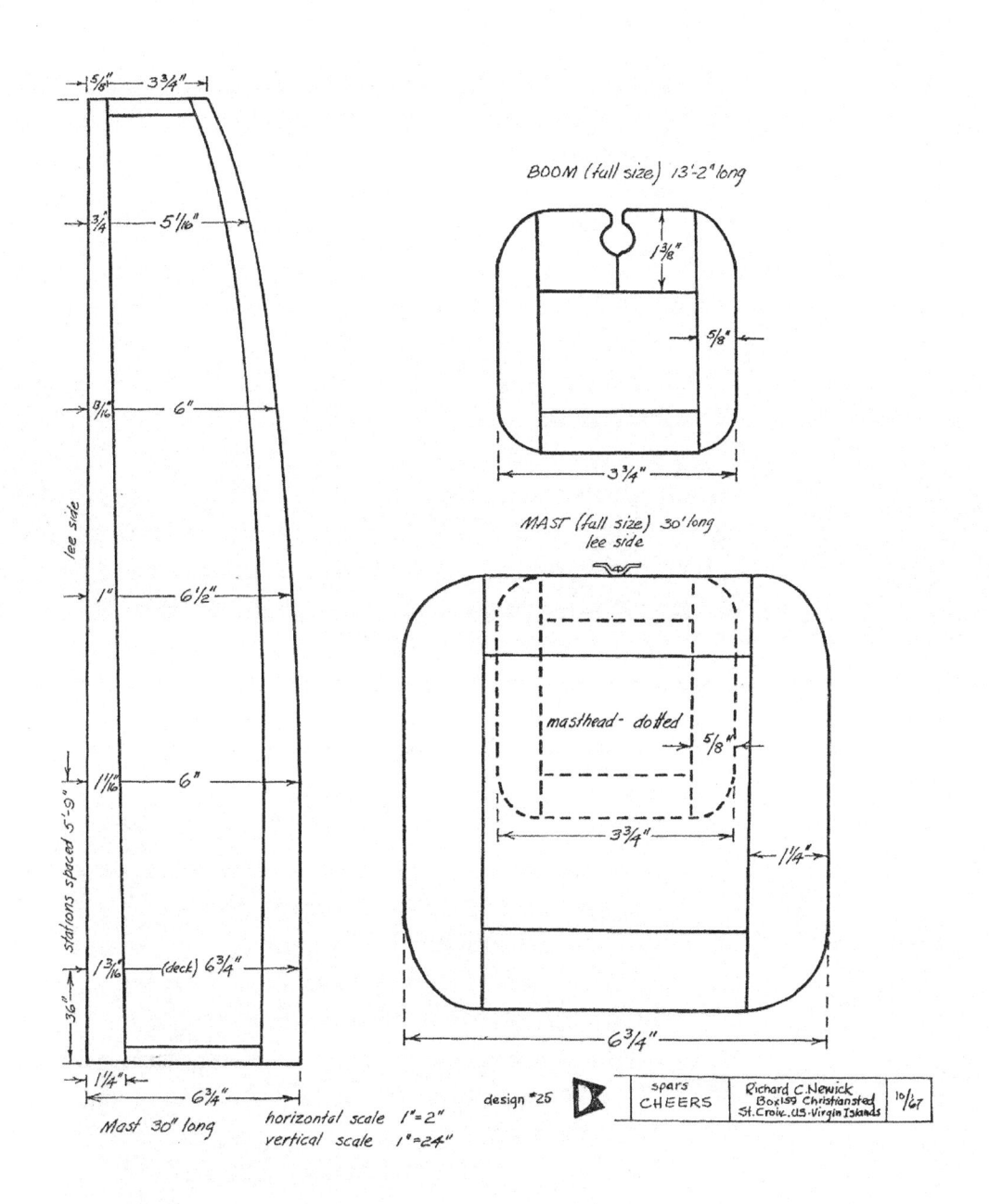

165

22. Tom Follett leaving Christiansted, St. Croix, Virgin Islands for England on 31st March, 1968. Photo Fritz Henle.
23. *Cheers* lying alongside her tender *Andiamo* at Millbay Dock, Plymouth prior to the Transatlantic Race. Photo Peter Wier

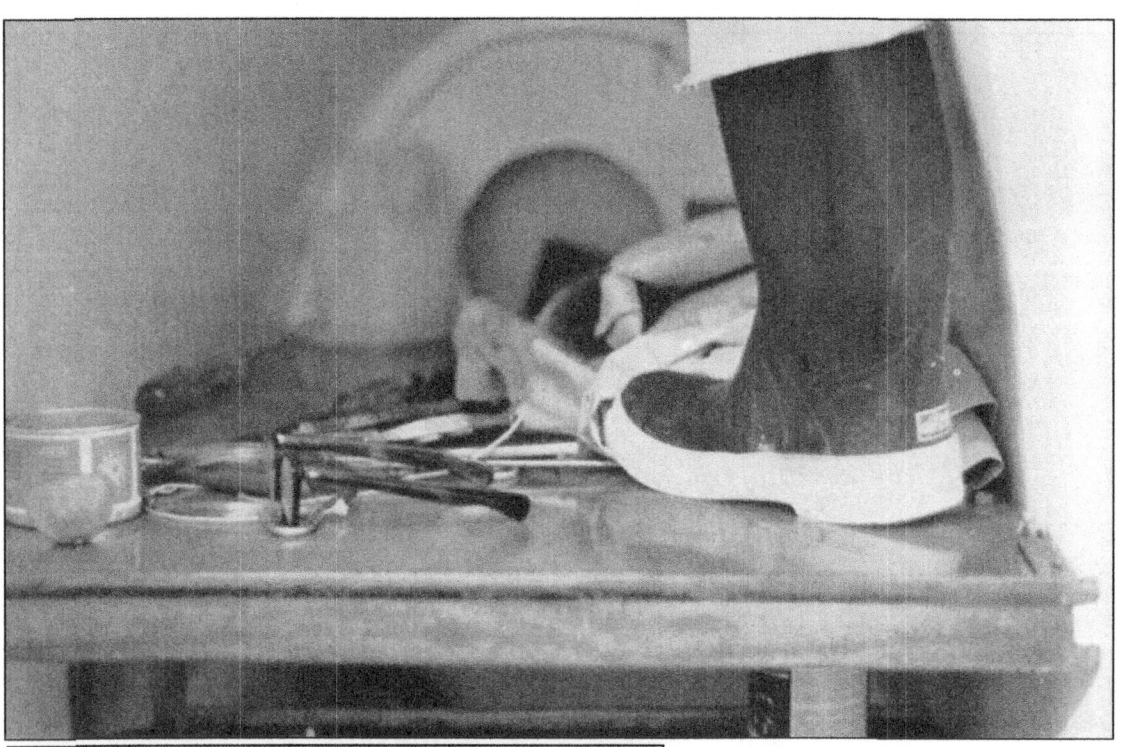

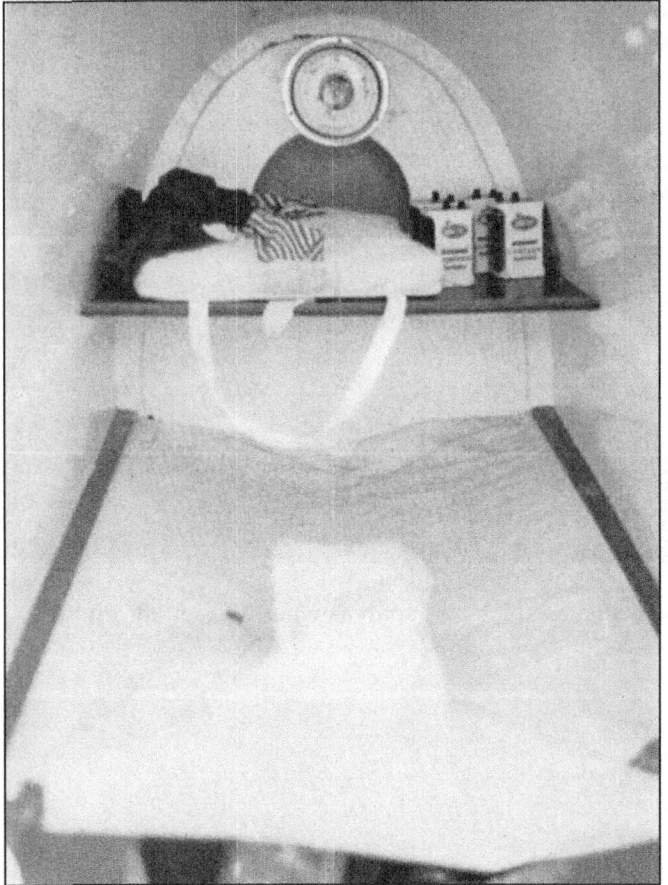

24. This shot shows the table opposite the berth.

25. Tom Follett's quarters for such long voyaging were cramped, to say the least. Here you see his bunk in the windward hull. Photo Peter Wier

26. Home after the race. *Cheers* looks just as spick and span as when she set off. Photo Newick

27. The contestants in the 1968 Single-Handed Transatlantic Race.

28. *Cheers* racing with Newick's third trimaran, the 36ft Trice, in some breeze. *Cheers* is considerably faster under these conditions. Photo Newick

Chapter three

First trials and the race

The launching was well attended with most able onlookers put to work lifting or pulling at one time or another. The old Polynesian ceremony of using live captives as rollers to launch their canoes through the surf was replaced by the pleasanter European custom of champaigne after Tootie Morris broke the first bottle over a bow.

Cheers set lightly on the water and was soon being towed through the pass in the reef with Tom, Jim and Dick slipping around on deck hoisting sail and clearing tangles of line.

In her element at last, and free of the towline, *Cheers* was easily driven by the moderate breeze, perhaps doing ten knots on a reach, but not pointing high enough to please us when going to windward. There was plenty for all three of us to do when 'tacking', which was the subject of some uneasy jokes about 'Newick's three man single-hander'.

'Tacking' isn't the right word; there doesn't seem to be a word in English for what we at first called 'the maneuver,' while awaiting the right word to fill the vacuum. This dilemma plagued us for some time. Betty Dickinson considered the problem while sailing with us and came up with the inspired creation 'tear' derived from a combination of 'tack' and 'wear'. Of course 'wack' would be an equally valid term, but the former is much more appealing.

Mr Kenneth P. Emory, Chairman of the Department of Anthropology at the prestigeous Bernice P. Bishop Museum in Honolulu advised us that there is no universal term among Pacific Islanders for the maneuver, but on the Micronesian island Ponape the term is 'rop'; at Nukuaro it is 'liki te ra' (te ra, the sail): and at Kapingamarangi they say 'hua te ra'.

So we will probably 'tear' or 'rop', 'liki' or 'hua' about until one term pushes itself forward to become a new English word.

Back to the beach for some obviously needed changes; replace the fancy stainless steel roller reefing goosenecks with old fashioned boom jaws for maximum flexibility, finish the daggerboard-rudders now that they seemed to do the job; place the winches, cleats, and fairleads so they would be most effective; tinker with steering linkage; and add spray rails to the bows; replace the boltrope slot on the masts with track and sew slides to the sails.

The weeks spent between trial runs at sea and alterations on the beach saw *Cheers* slowly evolve from a bundle of untested theories into sailing craft that self-steered on all points, and could be handled by one (good) man. She showed good bursts of speed, but still could not over take the 36-ft trimaran *Trice* except in strong winds.

The testing period had originally been scheduled for over six months. Late launching reduced that time considerably, but we still had a good four months to learn the boat's bad habits, and try to eliminate or minimise them. This process was absolutely essential to such a new and different craft. Without it we would not have wanted to send Tom offshore alone.

The first major test came in February when Tom loaded up perhaps 150 pounds of stores and equipment and headed for Barbados to do the 500 miles non-stop solo voyage that the Race Committee required for him to qualify for the race. By then Manfred had provided *Cheers* two mainsails, or a main and a foresail, if you prefer, plus three staysails that could be set flying.

The cockpit was snug under its new canopy, and the practice 'tacking' time had been reduced to just under a minute, except for handling a staysail if one happened to be set. Of course this was much more time than a conventional boat took to tack, but we hoped to be trading efficiency once underway for time spent maneuvering, which should increase our overall speed.

About the time we expected Tom back from his little cruise I got a phone call from him with the bad news that he had capsized, coupled with the good news that both he and the boat were all right, and heading home from Dominica the next day. What went wrong? He woke up swimming on a clear night in a moderate breeze a few miles in the lee of the high island of Guadalupe where unpredictable squalls were common.

Design and Construction

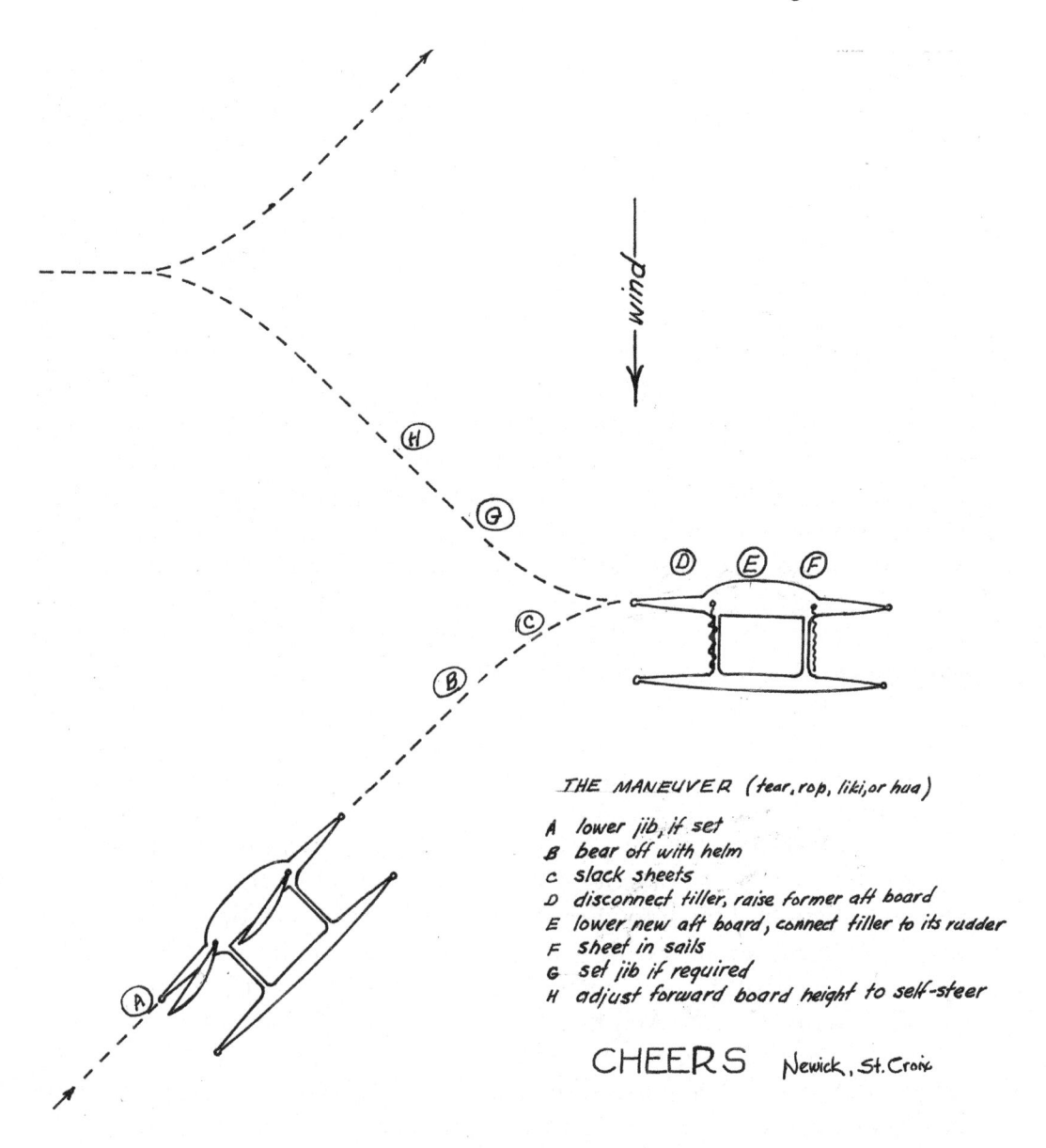

THE MANEUVER (tear, rop, liki, or hua)

A lower jib, if set
B bear off with helm
C slack sheets
D disconnect tiller, raise former aft board
E lower new aft board, connect tiller to its rudder
F sheet in sails
G set jib if required
H adjust forward board height to self-steer

CHEERS Newick, St.Croix

As proved earlier, the buoyant masts prevented the capsize from going beyond 90° but this was no help since Tom could not right the boat unaided. This was a capsize to 'windward', which we knew was our most vulnerable position. Having two thirds of the craft's weight in the windward hull coupled with her moderate sail area made it unlikely that she could capsize to leeward. Our concern was with the possibility of getting caught 'aback', and being blown over the wrong way. Early trials had shown this to be highly unlikely, but now it had actually happened.

As soon as Tom returned we took *Cheers* offshore in a stronger wind than she had when she capsized, put up the largest jib known as 'jolly green giant', and deliberately tried to capsize her by sailing 'aback'. It didn't work; we absolutely could not bring the ama, now to windward, up off the water. Several more days of light weather frustrated our capsize efforts so we hove her down in the harbor with buoyant fenders and life rafts lashed high on the weather hull to try to simulate the effect of proposed additional buoyancy in this area. We didn't learn much, but went ahead with the idea of a sponson, which would ordinarily be well clear of the water, but would sufficiently change the heeled buoyancy to facilitate self-righting, if not prevent capsize.

It bothered me that the several cures that suggested themselves were all rather heavy and awkward looking. Ian Major in St Thomas had been a helpful enthusiast right from the start of the project. After hearing of the capsize and studying Tom's report he suggested fastening the sheets so that they would automatically release themselves if they swung beyond the centerline. An ultra simple way to do this was found for the foresail. Still more assurance was needed, so the buoyant sponson was added high on the windward side. The sponson was built of ¼ in plywood without disturbing the basic hull structure and added considerably to its stiffness in the region of the cockpit, which had been too flexible when the boat was driven hard in a big sea. After covering with polypropylene and painting, the 'bubble' blended into the hull lines, providing an improved position for halyard and jib downhaul gear. Weight added was about 150 pounds.

Usually our Caribbean winters have several weeks of strong wind, but 1967-68 was an exception. We waited in vain for force 6 or 7 to give us a good test. One day with a moderate force 4 or 5, we managed to capsize her 'aback' after trying hard for an hour. With all sail set we found that only a touch of the helm or slacking of one sheet was required to bring the ama from a flying position, skimming the wave tops to windward, back down into the water; she did not want to go all the way over. The old Pacific Islanders certainly had something with their 'flying proas', but we still felt that our configuration was better for Tom sailing the North Atlantic alone.

Capsize 'aback' under these conditions happened quite slowly and deliberately. She did go on over until the spars rested in the water, in which position the sponson supported the whole of the rest of the hull clear of the water. First try at righting her with the skipper (still dry) stepping out onto a daggerboard brought her right back up, even without slacking the sheets. Left alone in a strong wind, I believe that the hulls would blow around to leeward at which time wind and wave would combine to right the boat. We never had the opportunity to test this.

After the capsize it became apparent that our only hope of convincing the Race Committee of *Cheers* seaworthiness would be to sail her to England, which Tom had originally proposed anyway. With the sponson doing its job and some certainty that every other component of the craft had been well tested, I had no reservations about anything except the cold weather Tom would find toward the end of his 4,000 mile journey.

Sheets and halyards were all of 3/8 in Dacron and showed little sign of wear. The whole rig was remarkably free of chafe, as a good deepwater rig should be, so Tom started out with most of the original running rigging. He had decided on a single burner gimbaled Sterno stove that burned solidified alcohol. On the first shakedown he discovered that a standard Primus stove was too much affected by the boat's short quick motion when sailing fast. By most standards, however, the motion was remarkably easy considering speed and the roughness of surface being traversed.

A simple table and a few shelves were added in one end of the cabin; a Dacron berth completed the cabin furniture. Two simple kerosene lamps were provided for warmth up north. One bucket was for the galley sink, another for the head.

The last additions were four ten inch diameter, 1/4 in aluminum discs bolted and screwed to the extreme ends above the spray rails at about 15° from the waterline. These, we hoped, would help the spray rails to provide dynamic lift when the bows started to dig into waves when going fast.

Project Cheers

The next time I would see Tom and *Cheers* would be in England. Only the experience of that voyage could tell us how much we would then have to do to prepare for the race.

At the Gosport, Camper & Nicholsons Yard, *Cheers* looked the same as when she left Christiansted, that is if anything could look the same under a leaden overcast instead of reflecting the blue, blue sky and white trade winds cloud of her home island.

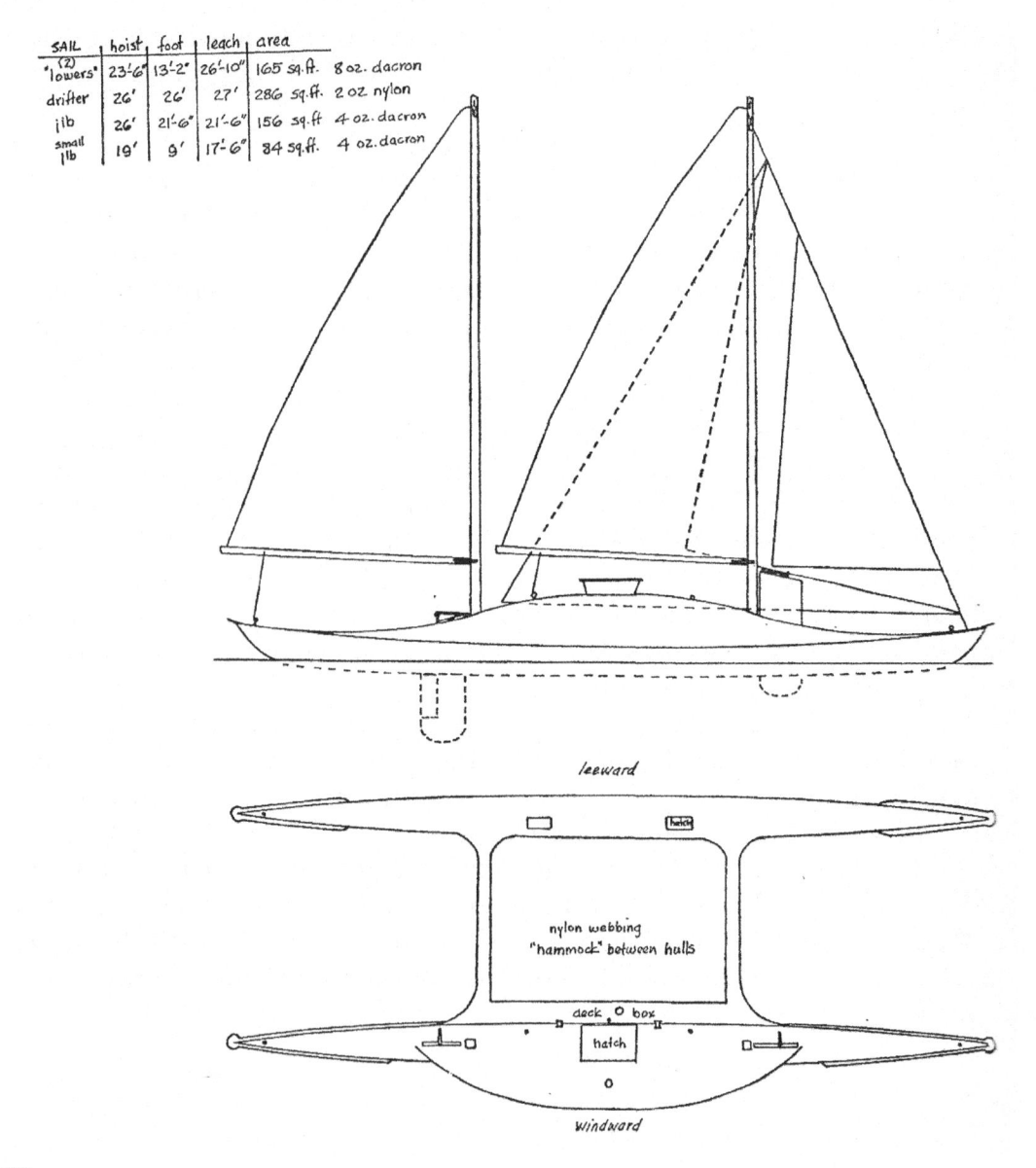

SAIL	hoist	foot	leach	area	
"lowers" (2)	23'-6"	13'-2"	26'-10"	165 sq.ft.	8 oz. dacron
drifter	26'	26'	27'	286 sq.ft.	2 oz nylon
jib	26'	21'-6"	21'-6"	156 sq.ft	4 oz. dacron
small jib	19'	9'	17'-6"	84 sq.ft.	4 oz. dacron

leeward

nylon webbing "hammock" between hulls

deck box
hatch

windward

Design and Construction

Tom told us that he had two problems on the voyage over that needed further thought. The bows still dug in when going fast in high seas, and the cabin was clammy with condensation in cold weather. Short of rebuilding the bows I could see no easy way to increase forward buoyancy without slowing the boat down, so we settled for a moderate increase in the size of the aluminum plates on the bows. Those that we had installed just before Tom's departure from St Croix were not reinforced, and had been bent up by the force of the sea, so obviously they had been helpful. The additions made at Camper & Nicholsons were adequately stiffened by two vertical webs.

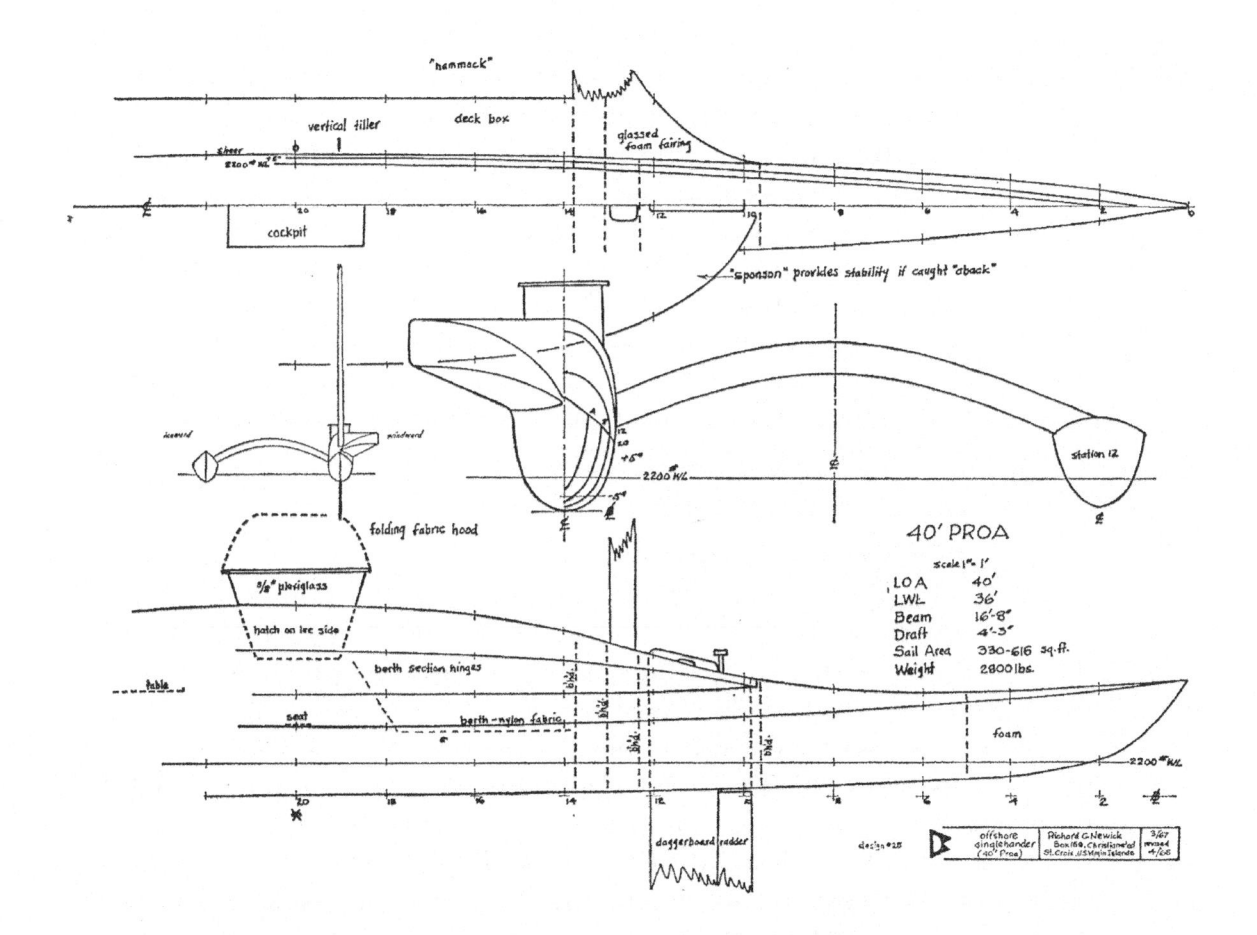

Pitch poling while driving hard before a steep breaking sea is a threat to any small craft. *Cheers* is vulnerable to the extent that the bows bury. Two and one half inch wide spray rails on the sheer line plus ten inch diameter discs at the very ends give noticeable dynamic lift, but the boat would demand careful handling in extreme conditions. Increased buoyancy is needed in the ends, probably in the form of more freeboard and overhang. It would be a shame to blunt the fine underwater lines that contribute so much to speed and an easy motion.

Another solution is to slow down, but a light craft such as *Cheers* has enough windage under bare poles to pick up considerable speed surfing down big seas in a gale. Slowing her down by towing lines decreases maneuverability and increases the danger of being pooped by a breaking sea, so the best all round solution would seem to be higher ends to enable reasonably fast downwind sailing in nasty weather.

Our only action on the cabin condensation problem was to sympathise with Tom. An inch of foam insulation would have been a comfort if such an item could be found in England, and if that inch of space all round the interior of the already small cabin could be spared. We did see a 1/4 in foam rubber lining that looked good on General R. H. Farrant's fine trimaran *Trifle* in Plymouth, but by then there was no time to procure and install it. No doubt the heat and sound insulation of even a half inch of the right material would have been considerable help in improving Tom's Spartan accommodation. Aside from temperature, the sounds of racing through the water at 10 to 15 knots are not conducive to rest when only 3/8 in of wood separates one's head from the sea.

Cheers' design, construction, and testing phases, each of which had taken six months were completed, giving us some time to observe the other competitors after we arrived in Plymouth. It was a fascinating fleet, probably as diverse as has ever raced offshore together. Most of the serious efforts to win were sponsored by commercial or even national interests. As we noted the size of the craft and the financial investments with which we were competing it became apparent that if little *Cheers* were to do well it would be because she was sailed by a seaman of Tom Follett's ability. One factor in his favor was our ruthless dedication to carrying only essentials. We were not displeased to see mountains of supplies and gadgets being stowed into other racers, knowing that every extra pound they carried would be a pound of water that had to be continually pushed aside every inch of the 3,000 miles from Plymouth to Newport.

The power to punch into the strong headwinds (and the highs seas they raised) made size a factor that would not have been so important with favorable winds. After studying the assembled fleet of competitors I found myself wishing that *Cheers* were perhaps ten feet longer. It was not until we actually saw the big monohulls that I realised how much of a threat they were in this particular race.

Eric Taberly's 65-ft trimaran was the favorite; obviously, if she could hold together and be controlled, the others were only racing for second place. Unfortunately, such pioneering needs more than the two weeks of sea trials that his tight schedule left him between launching and the start.

Joan de Kat, a Belgian artist, sailing his 50-ft trimaran *Yaksha*, which he had designed and built himself, had some fine ideas, but lacked the engineering to strongly tie his rangy craft together with wire stays. We discussed it, and agreed on simple solutions, but Joan, a very relaxed type, never got around to solving his problems.

French Commandant Waquet had designed two trimarans for the race, the 26-ft *Tamure* for himself, and the 40 ft *Koala III* for Frau Edith Baumann, who was the only woman racing. *Cheers* looked commodious compared with the twentysix footer. Edith Baumann's craft was more comfortable, but she herself hardly seemed at ease with the idea of a long solo voyage. Neither did we, after we heard of her lack of sailing experience. These two trimarans showed original thought in the design of the connecting structure, which looked both strong and light.

Bernard Rodriguez' 25-ft trimaran *Amistad* was the only other American entry that actually sailed. Like many of the other small boat sailors he has my admiration for doing a good job with little hope for reward except the pleasure of accomplishment. His trimaran, the lightest craft in the race, was an example of Arthur Piver's latest thinking.

The big Italian catamaran *Sail Giorgio* had an extremely strong rig and heavy gear -- the opposite end of the multi-hull spectrum from our lightweight *Cheers*. The work remaining to be done on her just a day before the start was shocking.

Project Cheers

As one observer in Plymouth said, we were watching two races, one to be ready to start on 1st June and the other to arrive first across the ocean in Newport.

We were lucky enough to be in Newport when the first five boats finished and had a chance to discuss the race with these superb skippers. They were already thinking about next time, and the concensus was that in 1972 it would take a larger boat to win. No skipper had a serious criticism of his boat or gear he used, but Bill Howell on *Golden Cockrel* observed that at speeds over ten knots, which were fairly easily achieved with his 43-ft catamaran, he did not feel safe leaving his wind vane self steering gear in charge of the boat. If more reliable self steering at high speed could not be devised he felt that he would want a large keel boat next time. He used a very ingenious electric sheet release device, which automatically uncleated any or all sheets whenever the boat heeled beyond a predetermined angle. This fine piece of engineering would have been useless if his power supply had packed up as Leslie Williams' had on *Spirit of Cutty Sark* in the middle of the Atlantic. Bill asked many questions about my thoughts on multi-hull design, but didn't seem prepared for the simple answer that they were there for all to see in *Cheers* .

Bruce Dalling pushed *Voortrekker* hard for second place. Her cold molded ply hull was built differently from *Cheers'* in that she had laminated frames. A few of these had cracked from the pounding, but this minor damage was more an indication of the beating she had taken than anything else.

The winner, Geoffry Williams, in *Sir Thomas Lipton* had a remarkably trouble free race, indicating extensive preparation and excellent design. Hull construction used a frame of iron pipe and angle iron at stress points, but the basic structure was a sandwich of foam covered with fiberglass and resin. Derek Kelsall has pioneered this in England and Jack Potter first used it in the States. We will probably see more of this strong, lightweight combination of modern materials, which lends itself to custom work such as this race encourages.

Cheers sail changes, Plymouth to Newport
1st June to 27th June 1968

'tear ' (change tacks)	31	times
mizzen set	29	" "
main set	14	" "
No 1 jib set	11	" "
No 2 jib set	18	" "
No 3 jib set	17	" "
foresail reefed	5	" "
mizzen reefed	2	" "

Tom and I discussed the rig and analysed his logged sail changes during the race. Many of the tacks were really not necessary Tom felt, so it seemed that our idea of concentrating on efficiency once underway rather than during the short maneuver was valid for a single-handed racer. Higher masts with a bit more sail area would probably be desirable now that we know what can be reasonably expected of one good man.

Study of these figures indicates that the three headsails were approximately the right sizes to keep *Cheers* going in moderate and light weather, but the one jib (genoa) would have been more effective if slightly larger and cut to set closer to the deck.

This one race, with the luck involved, does not 'prove' much, but might indicate some trends to watch in the future. So long as the rules do not limit size, cost, or sponsorship we can anticipate larger vessels requiring expert handling to realise their potential. Solo sailing at high speed is dangerous, especially in areas of poor visibility with much commercial traffic. I hope that ways can be found to make the race safer, but have been unable to come up with any suggestions that would not be somehow unpleasantly restrictive and counter to the welcome sense of freedom this race gives. The Royal Western Yacht Club Race Committee has the task of deciding what contender is fit to race -- a weighty decision! Perhaps they should invite some outside experts to share this load. England has many other men of experience who could give respected judgement. Perhaps the committee should even be made international.

Commercial sponsorship is unknown in American yachting, except for the unlimited hydroplanes that can soak up a great deal of money indeed. The average American sailor is quite horrified by the thought.

'Purity' is fine, but if commercial backing is the only way to get a certain dream off the drawing board, I can see where certain races, such as the Observer's Single-Handed Transatlantic Race, should allow sponsored craft.

Given a sensible approach, the sponsor should get a reasonable advertising return on his investment without offense. Our *Cheers* team of three may have had an advantage over the many lone individuals who were really single-handed from first effort to finish line. On the other hand, we were awed by others who were able to draw on vast resources for their efforts. We were proud to be the only one of the first five finishers that was without commercial or national sponsorship. The investment in *Cheers* was a small fraction of what many sponsors expended, and was also less than many of the individuals spent.

Col Hasler has seen the race he started in 1960 grow beyond anyone's expectations. His efforts, and those of the Royal Western Yacht Club and the *Observer* have broadened the horizon of all cruising yachtsmen. We owe much to 'Blondie' Hasler's quiet, sensible appreciation of the problems and the joys of sailing offshore.

The *Cheers* effort drew on many peoples talents. It was a privilege to have been a part of the group and to have known such worthy competitors in the race.

In my opinion the proa configuration merits further modern redevelopment. Remarkable returns await modest investments, but the usual pioneering troubles may be expected before we re-learn what the Pacific Islanders took for granted 400 years ago, as they sailed their light craft two or three times faster than cumbersome European vessels. One of history's sad misfortunes might be our ancestors' inability to learn from the islanders in boat design, and many other things as well.

Another proa has been pushing herself into my consciousness lately. (Where, oh where do these ideas come from?) She might be about sixty feet long, accommodate four simply, and should comfortably double the cruising speed of today's yachts. A small air cooled diesel could give her reliable close quarter maneuverability. Higher ends will enable her to keep sailing fast in a seaway. She will be recognisable as *Cheers'* big sister. But, no matter what comes in the future, *Cheers* will always have a special spot in the hearts of those of us who watched her grow.

Design and Construction

Project Cheers

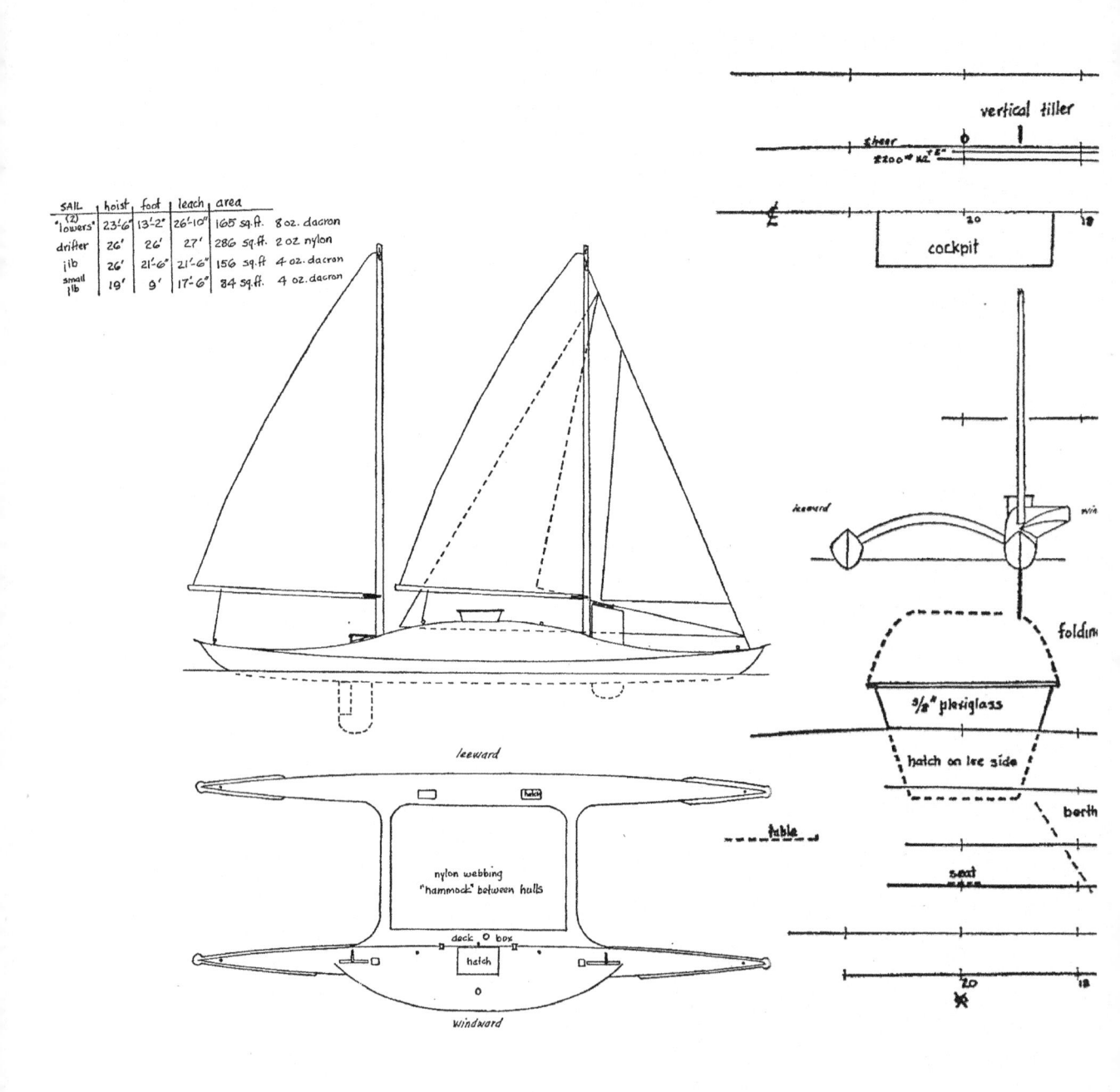

SAIL	hoist	foot	leach	area	
"lowers" (2)	23'-6"	13'-2"	26'-10"	165 sq.ft.	8 oz. dacron
drifter	26'	26'	27'	286 sq.ft.	2 oz nylon
jib	26'	21'-6"	21'-6"	156 sq.ft.	4 oz. dacron
small jib	19'	9'	17'-6"	84 sq.ft.	4 oz. dacron

Cheers in final form.

184

Design and Construction

"hammock"

deck box

glassed foam fairing

"sponson" provides stability if caught "aback"

windward

station 12

2200 WL

ng fabric hood

40' PROA

scale 1"= 1'
LOA   40'
LWL   36'
Beam   16'-8"
Draft   4'-3"
Sail Area 330-616 sq.ft.
Weight   2800 lbs.

th section hinges

berth - nylon fabric

bhd.

foam

2200 WL

daggerboard rudder

design #25

offshore singlehander (40' Proa) — Richard C. Newick, Box 150, Christiansted, St. Croix, U.S. Virgin Islands — 3/67 revised 4/68

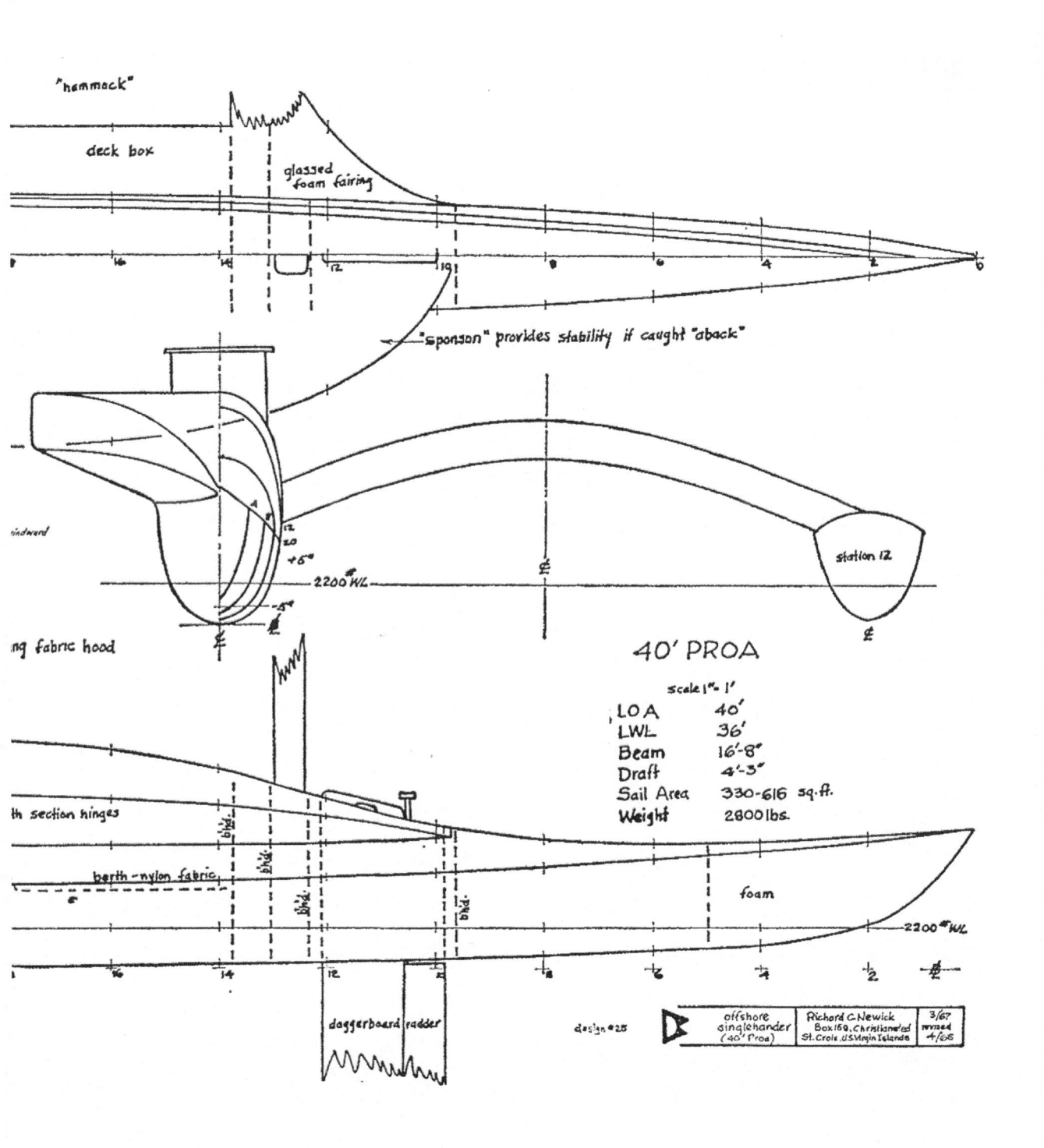

Project Cheers

Made in the USA
Middletown, DE
14 February 2022